FORCE Z SHIPWRECKS *of the* SOUTH CHINA SEA

HMS *Prince of Wales* AND HMS *Repulse*

FORCE Z SHIPWRECKS
of the SOUTH CHINA SEA

HMS *Prince of Wales* and HMS *Repulse*

ROD MACDONALD

Whittles Publishing

Published by
Whittles Publishing Ltd.,
Dunbeath,
Caithness, KW6 6EG,
Scotland, UK

www.whittlespublishing.com

ISBN 978-184995-095-4

Printed by Short Run Press Limited, Exeter.

Also by Rod Macdonald:

Dive Scapa Flow
Dive Scotland's Greatest Wrecks
Dive England's Greatest Wrecks
Into the Abyss – Diving to Adventure in the Liquid World
The Darkness Below
Great British Shipwrecks – a Personal Adventure

www.rod-macdonald.co.uk
www.authorsplace.co.uk/rod-macdonald
www.amazon.com/author/rodmacdonald

TO MY LATE GRANDFATHER CHARLES MACDONALD

CONTENTS

Acknowledgements

My thanks to Rob Ward of Illusion Illustration, Bridge of Muchalls, who created the stunning artist's impressions of the wrecks of these two great ships. Although we originally prepared illustrations after my 2001 Tri-Services Expedition, in writing this book and researching the ships more thoroughly we have been able to go on to correct and add more detail to the images. Any errors in the illustrations are mine alone – as Rob is not a diver and has never visited the wrecks. Rob also created the maps and other drawings throughout the book.

In preparing these illustrations we had to take a view as to how best to illustrate the complete wreck on a single page. The illustrations are impressions – not underwater photographs and out of necessity (to be visible to the reader's eye), some features had to be drawn larger than life and not to scale. These ships are immense and if everything was drawn to scale many details would be lost. A degree of artistic license has also been applied in places – such as with B turret at the bow of HMS *Repulse*, where perhaps the most photogenic aspect are the twin 15-inch gun barrels. These project through the sand from the buried turret Gun Room at an angle that would mean that the two barrels, 15-inches across would point directly at the reader – and never be seen in the illustration. Accordingly we have shown the twin barrels at a slightly different angle so the reader can see them.

Thanks also to (the then) Major Guy Wallis of the Parachute Regiment, who invited me as civilian expert onto the 2001 Tri-Services Expedition to survey these wrecks, and who has allowed me (again!) to use the fine photographs that he took as we explored the wrecks together.

To the late Ken Byrne, former secretary of the Force Z Survivors Association for his support and kindness; and the Imperial War Museum (IWM) for permission to reproduce archive photographs.

To Kevin V. Denlay, co-author of *Death of a Battleship: a Re-analysis of the Tragic Loss of HMS* Prince of Wales, for his assistance

Introduction

Just three days after the stunning raid by Japanese forces on Pearl Harbor provoked America's involvement in World War II, the brand new state-of-the-art, British battleship HMS *Prince of Wales*, and the mighty battlecruiser HMS *Repulse*, were attacked and sunk by 85 Japanese aircraft more than 130 nautical miles north of Singapore.

The two British capital ships had been left tragically exposed with no air cover, whilst as part of Force Z they sortied along with four destroyers almost 300 miles north of Singapore to try and interdict a rumoured Japanese invasion further north up the Malayan Peninsula. Both ships were hit by numerous torpedoes and bombs and had been sunk within 100 minutes of the battle beginning, with enormous loss of life. It was the Royal Navy's greatest loss in any single action.

Until this moment, the battleship had ruled the waves. It was the supreme embodiment of a nation's sea power and majesty. Heavily protected and heavily gunned, many considered them virtually unsinkable – although some had championed their vulnerability to air attack for decades. Battleships had already been sunk by other battleships, mines or torpedo, but the loss of HMS *Prince of Wales* was the first time that a battleship had been sunk by air attack in modern warfare. Its sinking is seen by many as marking the end of the era of the battleship, and the rise of the era of the modern aircraft carrier.

Prince of Wales was a brand new battleship; her hull was launched on 3 May 1939, but delays in her completion meant that she was not ready for action until 1941. In May 1941, when *Bismarck* and *Prinz Eugen* broke out into the North Atlantic intent on terrorising Allied shipping, the order went out from Churchill that the *Bismarck* should be sunk. *Prince of Wales*, one of Britain's newest and most formidable fast battleships, with ten powerful 14-inch guns, was tasked to take part in the search. Work to finalise setting up her gunnery systems had not been completed when she was ordered to sea for the hunt – and the civilian contractors working on her guns had to be taken along on the sortie.

Prince of Wales and Britain's most famous warship, the massive battlecruiser HMS *Hood* engaged *Bismarck* in a legendary battle, in which shells from *Bismarck* struck HMS *Hood*, completely destroying her in a cataclysmic magazine explosion which killed all bar three of her full ship's complement of around 1,000 men. *Prince of Wales* went on to land three crucial shots on *Bismarck*, even though one-by-one her guns, not yet fully operational, went out of action. One of the hits was serious enough to end *Bismarck*'s sortie and she turned for home as British forces concentrated for the kill. In the titanic struggle that followed, *Bismarck* was finally sunk.

Just months later, in late 1941, Japanese forces advanced into Indochina (the present-day countries of Cambodia, Laos and Vietnam) and started to threaten Malaya and Singapore. The Royal Navy had sought to have a Far Eastern Fleet created in addition to the Home and Mediterranean Fleets, but was stretched to the limit in Europe by the war against Germany. Churchill blocked the idea of a Far East Fleet and demanded that a small powerful naval force be sent to Singapore as a symbol of the might of the British Empire and to deter Japanese aggression. Force Z had been conceived.

Churchill's much beloved and newest battleship, *Prince of Wales*, would be sent along with the reconstructed World War I era fast battlecruiser *Repulse*. Admiral Sir Tom Phillips was chosen to command the squadron. An aircraft carrier was also tasked to provide air cover for the two British capital ships, but it ran aground in the West Indies and had to be repaired in America. It would not reach Singapore in time. Without its own air cover, Force Z had become dependent on ground-based aircraft cover from Malaya and Singapore. As they reached and entered Singapore on 2 December 1941 amid great fanfare, the two capital ships were in fact already exposed and almost indefensible, reliant on Fortress Singapore's own defences and poor land-based RAF aircraft rejected for service in the European theatre.

On 7 December 1941, the Japanese Fleet crept up on the American base at Pearl Harbor, Hawaii, and delivered their savage early morning attack. This devastatingly successful surprise attack crippled the American Pacific Fleet at anchor and triggered America's entry into the war. The same day, Japanese aircraft bombed Singapore and British Command realised that the Japanese would not be deterred from an invasion campaign by the presence of Force Z – no matter how powerful the two capital ships were. Reports arrived at British intelligence that the Japanese had started a land invasion 200 miles further north along the Malayan Peninsula at Kota Bharu.

At 5 p.m. on 8 December 1941, Force Z – comprising *Prince of Wales*, *Repulse* and four escort destroyers – set out to locate the invasion forces, if any, and attack them. It was a bold and daring plan that was reliant on monsoon rain and clouds to allow Force Z to arrive undetected with the element of surprise. They headed out into the South China Sea, hoping to surprise the Japanese forces at dawn on 10 December. The series of events that would lead to the beginning of the end of the battleship era now started to unfold.

En route to the possible invasion site, a signal was received advising that shore-based air cover – on which Force Z in the absence of its own carrier aircraft was now reliant – could not be provided due to heavy RAF losses from Japanese bombers attacking RAF airbases in the north of mainland Malaya. No plan survives contact with the enemy – and for complex reasons as the momentous events surrounding the Japanese invasion of Malaya unfolded, there were no RAF fighter aircraft patrolling above Force Z on its sortie. *Prince of Wales* and *Repulse* had become very vulnerable.

A Japanese submarine spotted Force Z as it steamed north towards Kota Bharu. Worse still, the poor visibility, which had shrouded the British warships as they sped to investigate, cleared just an hour or so before the cloak of darkness fell on 9 December – and Japanese reconnaissance aircraft spotted Force Z. Without air cover and now lacking the element of surprise, the two British capital ships and their escort destroyers belatedly turned and headed back for Singapore, making a night detour to Kuantan on their way south, to investigate further reports of troop landings. On learning of the presence of the British naval force, a Japanese night air-and-sea search located Force Z.

As dawn approached, Japanese reconnaissance aircraft were despatched from Saigon to sweep south in a large fan to re-locate the British Force. Once they were well on their way south, 85 Japanese bombers took off from Saigon, following slowly and waiting for reports from the reconnaissance aircraft of Force Z's exact location.

A Japanese reconnaissance aircraft spotted Force Z that morning, 10 December, at the end of one of its sweeps, and the armada of 85 bombers was directed to the location. They swooped down on the two exposed British capital ships in wave after wave of torpedo and bombing runs. As British anti-aircraft fire opened up, the commanders of the two British warships vigorously tried to comb the tracks of the torpedoes, turning their ships to face the oncoming torpedoes, so that they would pass harmlessly down the side of the ship.

Repulse, although struck by a single high altitude bomb that did little damage, evaded all the torpedoes of this first wave of attack. A single torpedo however struck *Prince of Wales* right at her most exposed point: her unarmoured Achilles heel around the port propeller shaft.

The most vital parts of a battleship are protected inside an armoured box called the 'citadel', and are almost invulnerable. But like any ship, to move through the water and navigate, the propellers and rudder have to be free and exposed to the sea. *Prince of Wales* had four huge propellers – two on either side of the hull at the stern. The single torpedo strike blew a hole in the hull right beside where the outboard port-side propeller came out of the hull – and at the same time, weakened the supporting struts that held the free section of the shaft in position. The outboard port-side propeller was driven by the forward engine, and the shaft ran more than 200 feet along inside the ship. With the supporting struts weakened, the propeller shaft vibrated until the supporting struts broke. The unsupported section of propeller shaft that projected outside the hull now corkscrewed around until the 17.5-inch-thick shaft itself broke, and a section of the shaft, along with the huge propeller itself, fell away, damaging the port inner propeller as it went and also forcing it out of action. Suddenly, from one critical torpedo strike, the great ship was reduced to her two starboard propellers for propulsion.

The thrashing of the shaft inside the ship caused massive damage internally to bulkheads and seals. Tons of water flooded into the hull through the gaping hole, searching through the damaged bulkheads of the shaft alley to the engine rooms. As she flooded with water into her port compartments, she settled by the stern and took over a heel to port. Electrical power to the stern part of the ship was cut off and both steering motors failed. Her rudder could not be turned – the ship could not be steered.

To trim the vessel, the crew tried counter flooding starboard side compartments. Despite the counter flooding attempts, the list to port caused the starboard side of *Prince of Wales* to rise up in the water, raising the vulnerable unarmoured hull beneath her armour belt, which was normally safely buried deep in the water.

Another wave of torpedo-bombers now swarmed at *Prince of Wales* on her raised starboard side, with some aircraft breaking off to simultaneously attack *Repulse*. With her rudder jammed, *Prince of Wales* could not manoeuvre and take avoiding action. She had lost power at her stern and some aft anti-aircraft guns could not function. Those anti-aircraft guns on her raised starboard side, that could still operate, could not depress sufficiently to counter the low flying torpedo-bombers streaking towards her only 100 feet above the water.

Repulse faced her own battle for survival bravely, but against overwhelming odds. At one point there were 16 torpedoes in the water, and her commander valiantly tried to manoeuvre his ship to comb the tracks. Finally however, her fate was sealed when a mass of Japanese torpedo-bombers attacked in a pincer-like star formation – torpedoes streaked towards her from every direction. *Repulse* couldn't comb all of these differing tracks, and she was hit by five torpedoes in rapid succession. Only 11 minutes after being struck by the first torpedo, she rolled over and sank quickly, with great loss of life.

Three torpedoes struck the now raised and vulnerable starboard side of *Prince of Wales* in quick succession. One hit her bow about 20 feet back from the stem – the blast blew right through her hull and out the port side. A second torpedo hit slightly forward of amidships under the protective armour belt, blasting into the unarmoured soft underbelly of the ship. The third torpedo hit the aft section of hull behind the armour belt, causing massive damage. She now had four holes in her hull – each some 7–10 metres in diameter – and a large section of her hull had been opened up to the sea. The end was inevitable. She slowly turned turtle and sank. Both capital ships were now on the bottom – Force Z had been destroyed.

Just a few days after the start of the war with Japan, and in less than 100 minutes of battle, Britain had lost two capital ships. It was the Royal Navy's greatest loss in a single action. Singapore would fall soon after to Japanese Imperial troops, with some 50–60,000 Allied soldiers being taken prisoner in the greatest ever capitulation of British-led forces.

Personal statement

Singapore: when I was growing up in Scotland it seemed an exotic place on the other side of the world, of no relevance to my life. And yet, slowly, I learned that my family had a strong connection with Singapore – and in particular to the Fall of Singapore in 1942.

My grandfather, Charles James Scott Macdonald, had been a Seaforth Highlander in World War I, having fought – and survived – at such bloody battles as Ypres and Beaumont Hamel on the Somme. The Highlanders were feared for their tenacious fighting by the German troops, who grudgingly admired them. The Highlanders went into battle wearing their kilts, earning them the nickname *Ladies from Hell*. My grandfather was decorated and received the *Croix de Guerre avec Palme*.

He was demobbed on 2 April 1919, returning from the battlefields of France along with hundreds of thousands of other troops at a rate of 15,000 men per week. He returned to his hometown, Elgin, in the north of Scotland, to find that there were no jobs and no money. Very quickly, in the same month he was demobbed – April 1919 – he responded to the advert below in *The People* looking for police recruits for the Shanghai Municipal Council Police Force. The Empire was calling to its demobilised working-class men. In 1919 alone, 200,000 men would leave Britain to take up posts in the Empire. By 1921, one million men would have taken up posts abroad.

OFFICIAL SITUATIONS

SHANGHAI MUNICIPAL COUNCIL, POLICE FORCE

POLICE RECRUITS are now required. Applicants must be unmarried, of good physique, with good teeth. About 20 to 25 years of age, not less than 5ft.10in in height, chest about 38in fully expanded, and able to furnish excellent references as to character. Salary commences at Taels 85 per month (at an average exchange equal to about £13 per month. The rate of exchange is liable to fluctuation). Men in the Army, Navy or Reserve must obtain full discharge before enlistment, AGREEMENT – for 3 years, with free passage to Shanghai: liberal superannuation scheme and bonus of £2 to outfit. Particulars will not be forwarded to applicants unless they clearly state in writing their age, height and chest measurements and that they are able to comply with the above requirements – Apply by letter in envelope marked "Police" to Messrs JOHN POOK and Co., Agents for the Municipal Council of Shanghai, 58 Fenchurch-Street, London EC3.

He went for interview – there were eight applicants for every post – but he was accepted. As a World War I sergeant he was used to discipline and command and would have been ideal. On 25 June 1919, he was sworn into the service and boarded the SS *Devanha* at Glasgow with the first batch of recruits. Leaving Scotland behind, the *Devanha* made its way through the Mediterranean, via Port Said and the Suez Canal into the Red Sea. She then crossed the Indian Ocean and called into Penang – the small island off the north-west coast of Malaysia, before running down the west side of Malaysia into the Malacca Straits and on to Singapore. From here she turned her bow northwards and headed up to Hong Kong, where the 34 recruits transferred to the China Navigation Company coaster SS *Tean* for the run up to Shanghai. He finally set foot on land in Shanghai harbour on 15 August 1919. Thirty-nine more UK recruits left Liverpool aboard the SS *Laertes* and arrived in Shanghai on 21 November 1919. The recruits were a motley collection of farm hands, plumbers, miners and working-class men who were viewed by the aristocracy of Shanghai colonial life as the lowest echelon of the British presence there – but nevertheless they were relied upon to act as the guardians of law and order.

In Shanghai, all the recruits underwent a period of training and familiarisation before taking up official duties as a Shanghai Municipal Policeman on the beat. Charles was soon promoted and joined the CID dealing with the war against the triads and opium gangs.

In 1925, he quit his job in Shanghai and got on a boat bound for New Zealand 'to better myself'. He jumped ship en route, in Singapore, where he found work on the P&O liners and rubber plantations, before eventually taking up a post as a prison officer at Changi Gaol.

As the Japanese invaded Thailand (then Siam) and northern Malaya in December 1941, and regular bombing raids were being made, it became clear that Singapore would fall. Along with thousands of other European families, his wife (my grandmother Iva Macdonald), along with my father Roderick Macdonald (then 11) and his two brothers, Gordon and Brian, were evacuated in January 1942 by the authorities on the now empty convoy vessels that had arrived with belated troop reinforcements for the Singapore garrison. Being a World War I veteran, my grandfather elected to stay behind in Singapore at his post as a Changi Gaol prison officer, as part of the civilian administration to help preserve order.

My grandmother, my father and his two brothers left Singapore Harbour at night under the cover of darkness in a ship already sporting bomb damage to its bridge superstructure. The ship left two hours before its scheduled departure time and took its chances, successfully running the gauntlet of Japanese aircraft. My family eventually made it safely back to Scotland by sea, after a lengthy stay in India.

My grandfather witnessed the increasing bombing raids and the siege of Singapore, writing to his family that the bombing was bad – but not nearly as bad as the World War I shelling he endured in the trenches. When the British forces surrendered, he was rounded up with the other Europeans in Singapore and marched off to internment, ironically in the very jail where he had been a prison officer.

The Japanese tortured many of the Allied POWs and civilian internees. They would hang people by their thumbs for days, or make them kneel, putting a plank of wood under and above their legs to cut off circulation. For more serious discipline, the Japanese would crucify prisoners by nailing them onto trees or a cross in the tropical sun. Others had dogs set on them. In my grandfather's case he never talked that much about what he endured except to say that the Japanese guards insisted that Europeans bow to them. Being old school British Army, my grandfather refused and was often beaten to the ground with rifle butts. I don't know what else happened to him, but he did suffer from early onset of dementia and the doctors treating him said it may well have been to do with his treatment at Japanese hands.

Japan formally surrendered on 2 September 1945. The Japanese guards at Changi disappeared and the prisoners were left to their own devices. On 3 September, two British destroyers *Cleopatra* and *Bengal* came into Singapore harbour, followed the next day by the cruiser *Sussex*. It came to light subsequently that the Japanese had informed British High Command (before the Hiroshima atomic bomb) that in the event of an attack on Singapore by Allied forces, all POWs and civilian internees would be executed. My grandfather was so ill from his three years of internment that he was taken to Singapore hospital, where it would appear he remained for almost a year before he was fit enough to return home to Scotland. During the years of incarceration my grandmother never knew if he was alive or not, as the Red Cross *Service des Prisonniers de Guerre* cards he filled out were held by the Japanese and not sent until after the war had ended.

In 2001, I was invited as civilian expert on a military expedition to dive and survey the wrecks of the two Force Z capital ships. A TV crew was aboard our dive vessel, filming the Timewatch documentary *The Death of the Battleship*. We spent a week filming each shipwreck and at the end of each week I was privileged to be present when the service personnel flew Royal Navy Ensigns on each wreck as a mark of respect and to honour their fallen comrades. It was extremely moving to be almost 130 miles north of Singapore and 50 miles offshore, hundreds of feet below the water, watching as British servicemen paid their respects. It was not lost on me that my grandfather, working in Changi Jail on 2 December 1941, would have watched as Force Z arrived – and how he would have been so shocked to learn of the sudden loss of these two ships.

On the wreck of *Repulse*, the Royal Navy Ensign was suspended from buoys on the spotting top. On *Prince of Wales*, the ensign was flown on buoys from one of the starboard side propeller shafts. A memorial plaque was also laid on the wreck.

When I returned, on a civilian expedition in 2005, it was touching to see that the ensign we had flown on *Prince of Wales* was still there in situ – groups of visiting divers had periodically renewed the buoys to keep the ensign flying in the underwater current, in memory of those lost.

Red Cross cards were filled out by prisoners to be sent back to relatives advising on captivity. These were retained by the Japanese and not sent in many cases. Author's collection

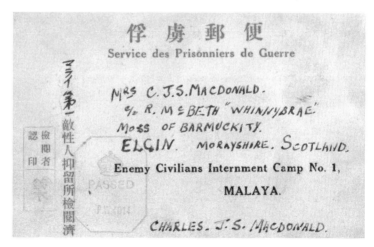

The officer in charge of the 2001 military expedition had liaised closely with the Force Z Survivors Association, who were helpful and supportive. They have a very active and helpful website at www.forcez-survivors.org.uk.

At the end of the 2001 military expedition, I was able to instruct the marine artist I have used for all of my shipwreck illustrations over the years, Rob Ward of Illusion Illustration, to produce the illustrations of the two wrecks in this book. To the best of my knowledge, this was the first time that anyone had made a serious go of illustrating the wrecks.

I was privileged to deal personally with the then secretary of the Force Z Survivors Association, Ken Byrne, who was very much onside with the aims of the expedition and was a complete old school gentleman to deal with. We had a number of lovely telephone conversations about the trip. He was interested in what his old ship now looked like and was able to recount some first-hand episodes from the action against the *Bismarck* – he had been serving aboard *Prince of Wales* at the time. I sent a number of prints of the two illustrations to Ken, as he indicated he was going to get two framed for presentation to an invited dignitary at the annual Survivor's Association reunion. I was invited to attend it but sadly could not.

A week or so after sending the prints to him, out of the blue I had a telephone call from Ken. He told me that when he opened up the package with the prints and saw the wreck of his old ship he started to cry. He had called his wife through to show her the print and said that after all these years, he was finally able to properly explain to her where he had been on the ship and what had happened on that fateful day in 1941.

It was moving for me to visit Changi Gaol itself and walk where my grandfather had worked, and where so much human suffering to POWs and internees had occurred. The museum staff there were very helpful and I sent a transcript of my grandfather's survivor account, along with prints of my wreck illustrations, to the museum for display.

There have been many historical accounts of the invasion of Malaya, the destruction of Force Z, and the Fall of Singapore – and this book does not seek to add to those fine books. But, to the best of my knowledge there has been no book illustrating the condition of the wrecks nowadays. To those that served on the ships, as they disappeared beneath the waves, it must have seemed like the end of the story; but to others, another story – of the life of the shipwreck – had only just begun.

Over the years, great interest has been shown in my illustrations of the two wrecks – non-divers find it difficult to visualize what shipwrecks are like and the wrecks are naturally hidden from view. So although I never set out with the intention of writing a book about the Force Z wrecks, I felt that by putting these images and knowledge of the condition of wrecks into the public domain, I was going a little way to preserving the memory of what happened and of those that perished.

This book is not intended as a dive guide – it is intended as a record of the story of these ships from the laying down of their keels, through the historical context in which they fought to the final tragedy of their loss and to the present day. The illustrations of the wrecks today are but a single snapshot in time of the life of these great ships. All shipwrecks decay and fall apart naturally over time, and in the decades to come, these ships will turn to dust and (barring the non ferrous parts), will disappear forever. I hope that my record of how the wrecks are today will be useful to posterity.

The author's grandfather Charles James Scott Macdonald in the trenches of World War I. Author's collection

Although much was written about the sinkings in the decades that followed the war, in recent years that swell of literature has dried up. The story is now getting more remote in time, and those that were involved are passing. But it is a very important story; fundamental in so many ways to where we are now, to Britain, to Singapore and to Malaysia. It touched my own life, yet for others – those that served and perished, those that survived, for the families of those lost – their lives were completely destroyed. Hopefully by writing this book, the story of those who fought and sacrificed will be brought to the fore again.

To understand a shipwreck, you need to know about the ship itself: its life and the historical context in which it existed. Without that knowledge, the wreck is simply a collection of metal at the bottom of the sea. To help provide that context, I have narrated a condensed summary of the Japanese problem in the 1930s that led to the creation of Force Z – and to the loss of the two capital ships off Malaya in 1941.

The sinkings and the subsequent Fall of Singapore caused a huge controversy at the time – a controversy that exists to this day. The battle has seen many, many detailed and fine investigations of what took place – and much blame has been apportioned. Although it has been necessary for me to recount the tragic story, I have purposely endeavoured not to get involved in the blame controversy. I have simply attempted to recount the story of what happened factually and in an easily readable fashion.

In so doing, I have learned a lot that is relevant to my own history. Singapore is part of my family history – if events had not turned out quite as they did, I would not be here to write this book.

BOOK ONE

FORCE Z CAPITAL SHIPS

CHAPTER ONE

BATTLESHIP AND BATTLECRUISER

A bit of background

Battleships such as HMS *Prince of Wales* and battlecruisers such as HMS *Repulse* were two completely different types of 'capital ship', from two different eras, that tragically found themselves under fire from a massed Japanese air attack that culminated in the ships sinking together in the far off waters of the South China Sea. That a battlecruiser such as *Repulse* could be sunk from the air was inconceivable at the time of her construction in 1916. When the *Prince of Wales* was launched in 1939, the threat of air attack was far better understood – but it was still generally felt that a modern battleship would be invulnerable to air attack. The loss of the *Prince of Wales* was the first time a modern battleship had been sunk in action by air attack. Her loss is often seen as defining the end of the battleship era.

Prince of Wales was a brand new, fast battleship, one of the five latest King George V-class battleships ordered by the Royal Navy in 1937 in the run up to World War II as the growing Nazi threat forced the Royal Navy to look inwards and realise its shortcomings. *Repulse* was a battlecruiser built in 1916 during World War I, but refitted in the 1930s.

Capital ships such as these two fine ships (and latterly, aircraft carriers) are the leading or primary ships in any navy: the biggest, most important ships. Slower, heavily armoured battleships had been around for a long time before even the idea of the fast, lightly armoured, all big gun battlecruiser was conceived just before World War I.

The British Royal Navy had been undisputed masters of the sea worldwide for more than 100 years before the great clash of steel warships at Battle of Jutland in 1916 – having come to a position of dominance during the innumerable maritime wars of the 16th, 17th and 18th centuries, as nations jockeyed for territory, colonial trade and raw materials.

At the beginning of the 19th century, in 1805, this rising ascendancy culminated in the Royal Navy's famed victory over the combined French and Spanish fleets at the Battle of Trafalgar. As Europe struggled to recover from the ravages of the Napoleonic wars, Britain used its maritime dominance to cement its Empire with new colonies established to protect and encourage lucrative trade. Britain's mastery of the seas was complete – and would be unchallenged for 100 years.

Towards the end of the 19th century, as Germany started to build up its own navy in a challenge to the traditional supremacy of the Royal Navy, a naval arms race developed. In 1906, the Royal Navy, under the charismatic leadership of First Sea Lord, Admiral of the Fleet Sir John Fisher, boldly embraced a risky radical alteration of the prevailing naval balance of power with the creation of a new type of battleship, HMS *Dreadnought*. She was such a new and powerful type of warship that she gave her name to a whole class of such new battleships – 'dreadnoughts'. Almost overnight, the generation of battleships that had gone before her was rendered virtually obsolete and classed as 'pre-dreadnoughts'. Soon, other major naval powers raced to build their own dreadnoughts.

The new dreadnoughts were a quantum leap forward in power and technology. They were about 10% bigger than the pre-dreadnoughts, and dispensed with much of the smaller calibre secondary armament to concentrate on being all big gun ships. The first of the new class of dreadnoughts were equipped with ten 12-inch guns set in five twin turrets, each gun being able to fire a 850-lb shell 18,500 yards (more than 10 miles).

The first dreadnoughts had three of the five gun turrets centered on the centre line of the vessel, two turrets forward and one turret aft. One turret was situated either side of the bridge superstructure in a staggered wing arrangement. With this initial arrangement, the new dreadnought could fire a broadside of eight shells to either side, six ahead and two astern. One dreadnought could match two pre-dreadnoughts for firepower at long range.

Before the dreadnought era, battleships and cruisers had no centralised fire control. Each gun was fired independently of the others from its respective turret. From 1906 onwards, battleships (and then battlecruisers) were fitted with the latest in range-finding techniques, sighting and fire control. Crucially, for the first time, all eight guns in a broadside could be aimed and fired by one gunnery control officer positioned in an observation post – or in a spotting top, halfway up the foremast.

The development of the dreadnought by Britain could have been a colossal own goal, by destroying her traditional naval supremacy in the balanced order of the time. But taking the calculated view that British shipyards could build more of the new dreadnoughts than the shipyards of any rival countries, the Royal Navy gambled with the launch of HMS *Dreadnought*. They gambled – but won. By the start of World War I in 1914, Britain had 22 of the new dreadnoughts in service, compared to Germany's fifteen. Britain also had another 13 under construction compared to Germany's five.

Armour

Battleships

Battleships protected their most important and vulnerable parts inside an armoured box called the 'citadel', which ran from just in front of the forward gun-turrets all the way back to aft of the stern gun-turrets. Along the side of the citadel on either side of the ship at the waterline, ran the main vertical armour belt, which was 11 inches thick in the first dreadnoughts but gradually got thicker with successive new classes of battleship. By World War I, German standard main armour belt was 13.8 inches thick.

In front of the forward gun-turrets and aft of the stern gun-turrets, an armoured bulkhead crossed the ship athwartships, from one side of the hull to the other, connecting the vertical armour belts on both sides of the ship to form the rectangular framework of the citadel. The main deck had a layer of armour on it and there were further armoured decks deep within the ship to protect the magazines at the very bottom of the ship.

When the first generations of steel battleships were developed, the less powerful guns of the day had a restricted range, and so fired in a relatively flat trajectory from relatively close range. A typical range would be 6,000 yards with a long range engagement being 10,000 yards. At short range, a shell that followed a flat trajectory reduced the fire control problem of compensating for the roll of the ship whilst pointing the gun at the target. This proximity and low trajectory meant that shells fired were more likely to hit the side of the enemy ship, which was protected by the vertical armour belt. The shell would not strike the deck, and so to save unnecessary weight, decks were more lightly armoured than the vertical side armour belt.

Soon however, as battleships developed, successive generations of new and improved big guns could hurl their shells further and further. Soon shells were being fired with a range of 21,000 yards – some 12 miles. More powerful guns firing from greater distances increased the height of the shell's trajectory and produced a new phenomenon: 'plunging fire' or 'falling shot'. This was likely to strike the more lightly armoured deck of a battleship, rather than the thick side armour belt. The first dreadnoughts had deck armour just 0.75–3 inches thick. This was thickened as the battleship evolved and by World War I, German battleships had 3.8-inch-thick deck armour.

Battlecruisers

First Sea Lord Sir John Fisher, who had master minded the development of the new breed of dreadnought battleship, strongly believed that speed was the most effective form of defence, and instigated the development of a new type of armoured cruiser: the battlecruiser. The new battlecruiser would have eight big 12-inch guns, as on a battleship, but instead of the thick armour plating of the dreadnought, they would be more lightly protected, relying on their exceptional speed of 25 knots (later classes would have speeds of 32 knots) to take them clear of danger. The first battlecruiser, *Invincible*, was completed in 1908 and was fitted with vertical main belt side armour belt just 4–6 inches thick and deck armour 1.5–2.5 inches thick.

Fisher's new battlecruisers had a several-knot speed advantage over dreadnought battleships and all armoured cruisers. The extra speed, Fisher believed, would offer the protection that their light armour could not. Battlecruisers thus possessed the speed and firepower to hunt down and destroy the most powerful armoured cruisers of the day, while their speed also gave them the option of withdrawing from action and outrunning any battleship they may encounter. Both sides however, largely forgot this basic premise when World War I erupted and lightly armoured and vulnerable battlecruisers found themselves pitted in action directly against far more heavily armoured battleships in a one sided contest.

The 12-inch firepower of the battlecruiser big guns seduced naval commanders into using them as the fast wing of the battle fleet – and this brought them into first-contact with the heavy calibre shells of enemy dreadnoughts. The frailty of the battlecruiser was tragically exposed at the Battle of Jutland on 31 May 1916, when the battlecruisers HMS *Indefatigable*, HMS *Queen Mary*, and HMS *Invincible* were struck and blew up in catastrophic magazine explosions with the instant loss of almost all of their individual crews.

Armament

British battleships generally carried larger guns than their German opponents, giving greater firepower. German designers, however, emphasised protection at the expense of firepower. In time, as battleship-design evolved, construction of British dreadnoughts became constrained due to the limiting size of existing British dry docks, which made an increase in beam impossible. German shipbuilders had no such restrictions, and so their battleships possessed a greater beam, which allowed for increased protective measures such as greater sub divisions and torpedo bulkheads.

The first German dreadnought battleships were equipped with the traditional German 11-inch gun, which had a high muzzle velocity and gave outstanding range. The 11-inch gun, however, fired a relatively small shell, which had limited penetration.

In the second class of German dreadnoughts, a slightly larger 12-inch gun was fitted. The Germans initially held to this 12-inch shell, despite the British move to a 13.5-inch, and then finally to a 15-inch shell. But by the closing years of World War I, new German battleships under construction were being fitted with 15-inch guns.

Battleships and battlecruisers were essentially armoured floating platforms to deliver shells from their big guns – the guns being the *raison d'être* for these steel titans. The gun turrets, being so crucial, were heavily armoured, with the heaviest armour being on the turret face and sides – some 11–12 inches thick on some ships. The same thinking that had given vertical side armour belts great thickness but left decks lightly armoured, carried forward to the turrets, where unlike the thick sidewalls, the turret roof was only given 3–4 inches of armour to protect against splinters from shells bursting above. Turrets too became vulnerable to plunging fire, as the range of big guns increased.

The British initially equipped their first dreadnoughts with 12-inch guns, which had a rate of fire of approximately two rounds per minute per gun. At long range it was found that the latest version of this gun, which dated back to 1893 (but now had lengthened barrels), had accuracy problems. To solve this problem, the Royal Navy quickly went to the 13.5-inch gun, beginning with the 'Orion' class of dreadnoughts. This larger gun allowed for a much larger shell, which gave improved penetration. The larger shell and increase in bore allowed a lower muzzle velocity, therefore giving much greater accuracy and less barrel wear. The final development of the pre-war British dreadnought was a 15-inch gun, which was reliable and accurate with a low muzzle velocity that gave outstanding barrel life. *Repulse*, being built in 1916, was fitted with the new 15-inch guns.

All British turrets had a rangefinder installed at the rear of the turret, designed primarily as a back up if the centralised fire control system failed. However, the provision of additional rooftop sighting hoods on British turrets made the gun crew susceptible to blast damage if a superfiring turret fired over it.

The two forward turrets on Royal Naval vessels were called 'A' and 'B' turret and the two aft turrets 'X' and 'Y' turret. If there was a waist-turret aft of the bridge, it was called 'Q' turret. German turrets used the German phonetic alphabet (although they did vary slightly from ship to ship), and were usually called '*Anna*', '*Berta*', '*Cäser*' and '*Dora*'. Like the British turrets, all German dreadnought main battery turrets were provided with a rangefinder on the turret roof.

The ammunition for the big guns was kept in magazines situated at the bottom of the ship, where they were protected by their depth in the surrounding water and by armoured decks above them. In all, there were about 50 magazines in the German ships, which were protected against torpedoes by longitudinal bulkheads of strong nickel steel.

Gunnery

The task of hitting an enemy warship was complicated and difficult, requiring huge manpower involvement from the crew and the latest technology for the time. To get a perspective on how hard it was, during World War I, the opposing ships would be manoeuvring at their top speed of about 23 knots on battleships and 25–30 knots on battlecruisers. They could be 10 miles or more apart, and if steaming at full speed towards each other would have a combined closing velocity of 50–60 knots. Imagine trying to fire a shell 10 miles and hitting something that is coming towards you at 60 mph. To increase the complexity of the task, the ships would often be fighting in the stormy waters of the North Sea, pitching and rolling in its notorious swell. One minute your guns could be pointed at the enemy, the next they could be pointed into the sea. Sudden changes of course and alterations in speed were made by both sides to try and avoid the hail of high-explosive shells coming from the distant horizon. Hitting another ship was extremely difficult.

By the outbreak of the World War I, the Royal Navy fire control system on capital ships had become very elaborate, with the use of a 9-foot-wide Barr & Stroud rangefinder to measure the distance from the gun to its target. This rangefinder was technically capable of providing accuracy to 85 yards at a distance of 10,000 yards, but, as was later proved at Jutland in 1916, the accuracy of the rangefinder was much reduced in action due to light refraction and the heating of the rangefinder tube.

A rangefinder provided the 'true range' to a target – not the 'gun range'. To calculate the gun range it was necessary to factor in and compensate for:

(a) the enemy vessel's movement throughout the water and;
(b) the ship's own movement.

To do this, the Royal Navy initially adopted an analogue-computing device, called the 'Dumaresq' after its inventor. The 'range rate' information from the Dumaresq was transmitted to the guns electromechanically by means of a Vickers receiver-transmitter.

In 1912, the Admiralty adopted the Dreyer Fire Control System, which allowed operators to visually compare ranges reported by rangefinders to a continuously evolving estimate of the range rate being sent to the guns. 'Dreyer Tables' were sturdy iron tables fitted with a number of fire control devices, operated by rotating shafts, chains and linkages and worked simultaneously by seven or more men. They were essentially complicated early mechanical computers, but they suffered from a number of limitations. The Dreyer Tables were replaced by the much better 'Argo Clock' in the early years of World War I – but only a few British ships had the new system by the time of Jutland.

The Royal Navy developed a centralised Admiralty Fire Control System, which relied on a device called 'the director' – usually fitted in the foretop – the armoured conning tower, or 'director control tower', situated immediately behind B turret. The top of the director control tower held a revolving chamber with a circular base. Optical rangefinders mounted on top at its back, protruded from either side. From here, the guns were directed, controlled and fired.

The conning tower was a feature of most battleships and cruisers from the late 19th century until the early years of World War II. Although, when not in action, a capital ship would be navigated from the bridge, the conning tower (located at the front end of the superstructure) was a heavily-armoured cylinder, varying on different ships from 4.5 inches to 12 inches thick, with tiny slit windows on three sides providing a field of view for officers during battle. It was also fitted out to allow navigation during battle, with engine order telegraphs, speaking tubes, telephones and helm. The conning tower developed in the Royal Navy to become a massive structure weighing hundreds of tons – but Royal Navy analysis of World War I combat revealed that officers were unlikely to use the conning tower during battle, preferring the open superior views of the unarmoured open bridge. Older Royal Navy ships that were reconstructed with new superstructures had their heavily-armoured conning tower replaced with lighter structures.

By World War II, gunnery systems had improved dramatically. The captain of a Royal Navy ship would select the enemy to engage using a device called 'the captain's sight'. When the crew of the director control tower received an indication of the enemy target from the captain via 'the captain's sight', the revolving top section of the tower was trained round until the target selected by the captain could be seen. This gave the bearing of the target, and this bearing was then sent to the guns electrically. The guns were then all automatically trained on the same bearing as the director control tower.

The bearing of the target was also sent by the director control tower to the transmitting station – the gunnery nerve-centre of the ship, deep down inside the citadel and protected by its horizontal and vertical armour. Here, the 'aim-off', or additional training movement required to hit the enemy, would be calculated and sent to the guns, which were then pointed in slightly a different direction to the director control tower. The Admiralty Fire Control Table also sent to the guns the movement in elevation required by the range of the enemy (calculated initially by optical range finders and latterly by radar).

The guns were now pointed and elevated correctly, and would be fired by the director layer. The director layer sat in the front position of the revolving top section of the tower, looking through a telescopic sight (the 'director sight') at the enemy. Beside the director layer sat the director trainer, whose job it was to train the tower on the target and keep it trained as the target moved. As the guns became loaded and ready to be fired, individual 'gun ready' lamps lit up in the transmitting station. As soon as all the 'gun ready' lamps showed 'READY', the transmitting station pressed a button on the Admiralty Fire Control Table, and this rang a gong in the director control tower. When the gong was heard, the director layer pressed a pistol grip trigger as soon as he was on the target, and all the guns were fired simultaneously by electric current.

The director thus enabled all the ship's guns to be trained, laid and fired from a single position. The training-angle and elevation for the guns was transmitted electronically from the director to each of the turrets, where the desired settings were laid automatically by the control systems in the turret.

The World War I German ships did not have as sophisticated a fire control system as the British, but at Jutland their system proved at least as effective as the British system. In German ships, a gunnery officer was in charge of the guns, and under his control would be a number of officers and about 750 men all dedicated to the process of firing. More than half the crew were assigned to the gunnery system when the ship was in action.

The fore control in German ships was an armoured chamber, which formed the rear portion of the conning tower and from which the captain, supported by the navigating officer and the signal officer, navigated the ship in action. The gunnery officer or director layer was supported by three lower-ranking gunnery officers (who controlled the secondary battery), men on the range finder, men on the director, and by a number of men for transmitting orders. Immediately below and often separated only by an iron grating on which they stood, more messengers stood waiting. In all, there would be more than 30 men in the fore control, which was armoured sufficiently to withstand a hit from a 6-inch gun at short range.

Both sides had two other controls in addition to the fore control: the 'after control', where the secondary gunnery officer had his post; and the 'spotting top', well up the foremast. The spotting top was a small armoured chamber with viewing slits around it, in which the observer for the main armament, a lieutenant and the spotting officer for the secondary armament, were stationed, along with other officers and messengers who observed the splashes from the fall of shot around the enemy and transmitted corrections to the gunnery officers through head telephones.

Although fire control systems varied from nation to nation and ship to ship, it was common for all orders from the gunnery officer or director layer to go by telephone and speaking tube to a transmitting station situated beneath the armoured deck below the waterline at the bottom of the ship. From there, orders and information were transmitted to individual guns.

Early German capital ships had up to seven large 9–10-feet wide stereoscopic rangefinders, which gave excellent results up to 12 miles or more. Each rangefinder housed and was operated by two men: one who took the range while the other read off the distance and set the figures on a telegraphic indicator. This indicator delivered those figures to another transmitter, which automatically sent the figures given by all seven range finders. The average of the ranges given by all the instruments could be read off by the gunnery officer, who gave the range to all the guns.

As soon as the gunnery officer had selected an enemy ship to fire at, he would focus the cross hairs of his periscope sight on that ship (on German ships it was the same periscope as on a submarine). This allowed the small observation slits in the armoured conning tower to be completely closed by armoured caps.

A director was situated on the periscope of the gunnery officer, and this enabled all the guns of the ship connected to the director to follow every movement of the gunnery officer's periscope. Guns more than 100 metres apart at bow and stern could be trained on exactly the same spot 12 miles away, in the direction fixed by the periscope – the distance of which has been established by the rangefinders.

Where the director was in operation, the guns were kept on the enemy, without any crew actually working the guns needing to see the target. The director operated an indicator in every turret, which gave all the corrections for range and deflection. The enemy could be close or far away, ahead or astern, the ships could be passing each other side-by-side. As long as the periscope is on the target and as long as the proper range – or distance to the target – has been established, each gun is aiming at exactly the part of the enemy ship that the periscope is pointing at. Even when the ship turns sharply, so long as the periscope is kept on the enemy, all the guns remain on target.

Once the range was known, the guns themselves had to be elevated or lowered according to the range. In the transmitting station, deep in the bowels of the ship, was situated an 'elevation telegraph'. When the telegraph was moved to the desired elevation, an 'elevation repeater' or 'indicator' on each gun (linked to the elevation telegraph) moved to the figure indicated by the elevation telegraph. This worked in much the same way as when a telegraph on a ship's bridge was moved to Full Speed or Half Speed, a repeater in the engine room connected by chain to the bridge telegraph would ring up the required instruction.

The elevation repeater moved an indicator on the gun sight and the gun was trained to the proper elevation. The gunnery officer operating the director on his periscope-sight provided the necessary firing impulse for a simultaneous salvo from all the big guns from a pistol-type firing mechanism.

The 'range clock' was sited on the elevation telegraph. If the gunnery officer had calculated that the range to the enemy was decreasing by say 750 metres per minute, an order would be given – "rate 750 minus". The range clock was then set at a speed of 'minus 7.5' and the range given on the elevation telegraph gradually diminished by that amount. The indicator on each gun changed automatically without the necessity of giving any orders.

The gun now had the required elevation and was trained accurately on the enemy by the periscope. But the ship could be rolling heavily – one minute the guns could be pointed at the water and the next minute they could be pointed at the sky. The 'gun-layer' was tasked to ensure that the sight of the gun was always kept trained on the enemy. This was a drill practised almost daily by both sides, to hone individual skills. Even when the ship was anchored in port, gun layers could practice shooting from a rolling ship – small targets could be moved around in front of the ship: the target would move on curves, which correspond to the rolling of the ship, but the ship and its guns were stationary.

After Jutland, warships developed a device which automatically enabled the loaded gun to be fired at the moment when the telescopic sight was on the enemy.

The upper part of the main turrets, called the 'gun room', consisted of a heavily-armoured revolving turret and the revolving platform on which the guns were situated – all turned by electricity. The ammunition hoists also emerged close to the guns and turned as the turret revolved, the hoists descending down to the magazines deep in the bowls of the ship, inside an armoured cylinder called a 'barbette'. Behind the guns was a relay of ready ammunition, about six rounds for each gun.

Shells & propellant

There were two types of shell: armour-piercing and high-explosive. The Germans painted their armour-piercing shells blue and yellow during World War I. These were made of the best nickel steel and had only a small high-explosive charge. The object of the shell was to pierce the enemy's thick armour and then burst inside.

The high-explosive shell was painted all over yellow by the Germans, had a comparatively thin steel case and contained a large amount of high-explosive. This shell could not penetrate thick armour but its huge explosive effect was devastating on unarmoured or lightly-armoured targets.

The Germans held their powder in brass cases. The 6-inch cartridge looked exactly like a giant sporting cartridge. These large brass cases were difficult to manufacture, were expensive and extremely heavy, but notwithstanding these drawbacks, the German Imperial Navy used these brass cases even for the heaviest calibres. This careful practice saved them from catastrophes such as the magazine explosions of the British battlecruisers *Indefatigable*, *Queen Mary*, *Invincible* and the older armoured cruisers at Jutland. The necessary amount of powder required for a large-calibre main gun could not be contained in a single brass case, so in addition to the main brass cartridge the Germans used a secondary cartridge – the powder for which was contained in a double silk pouch. These naturally caught fire easier than the brass cases.

During World War I, the British kept all their powder in silk pouches and used light, flash-proof 'Clarkson cases' as cordite propellant-charge containers for transit – the silk pouches being placed in the Clarkson cases before they left the magazines. The Clarkson cases then rode up the hoists to the guns where the charges were removed when it was time to load them into the breach. The now-empty Clarkson case was then returned to the magazine for re-loading. The silk pouches were thought to represent a considerable saving in weight and magazine space, compared to brass cartridge cases.

The Germans kept all their cartridges, which were not by the gun or on the ammunition hoists, in tin canisters so that they could not easily catch fire. With a view to minimizing the dangers of a flash-fire and catastrophic explosion, German orders were that only one secondary and one main cartridge were to be kept on the platform by each gun, and the same rule applied on the lower tiers of the platform.

The revolving gun turret rotated on the fixed armoured barbette – a cylindrical armoured tube some 30–40 feet wide that reached down through several decks and had the armoured deck at its base. The interior of this barbette was divided into several tiers: the transfer room; the switch room; the magazine; and the cartridge magazine. In all, including the gun room of the turret and the barbette, the structure was some five stories high and housed 70–80 men.

The function of the transfer room was to send ammunition up to the guns. A small stock of ammunition and cartridges was kept in the transfer room, which thus became the reservoir from which the gun was supplied – and not the magazine directly.

There were no hoists running right through to the turret in the German ships. The lower magazine and cartridge ammunition hoists were connected to the transfer room, and from here the shell or cartridge was sent to the gun. However, the safer German system of transfer slowed down the process of getting shells from the magazine to the guns, but two rounds of cartridges for each gun were simultaneously on their way in the German ships. In British ships, flash-proof doors were designed to stop explosive gases reaching the magazine in the event of a hit on a turret, and explosion-proofing was one of the main features of the barbette. However, the British stressed rate of fire as being paramount to smother the enemy's sight lines and ability to return fire. Safety precautions were compromised: the shell hoist system was more direct and in the early days, propellant-charge handling was more lax, with multiple charges being stacked around outside the flash-proof turret protection.

Even with their more complicated system, each German gun could fire comfortably every 30 seconds – and they could fire a single gun every 15 seconds (instead of both guns). They often fired a salvo of 4 single shells, one from each turret every 20 seconds.

Torpedo & mine protection

Up until 1905, normal battle-ranges for capital ships were assessed at 6,000 yards, with long-range engagements perhaps out to 10,000 yards. At both these ranges, the shell of a high velocity gun would strike its target's side. For this reason, a capital ship's armour was concentrated on its vertical main belt along the hull side at the waterline, and designed to protect the ship's vital areas, such as magazines and propulsion spaces. The main belt ran from forward of the forward turrets to aft of the aftmost turrets.

German ships were built with a higher emphasis on protection than Royal Navy ships, and so their armour belt was usually thicker than British armour belts. Since it was believed that heavy shells would not have the trajectory to strike the ship's horizontal areas, such as the deck or turret roofs deck, armour there was comparatively light – designed primarily to provide protection against splinter damage from shells bursting above.

The real danger to dreadnoughts was the advent of reliable torpedoes and mines during World War I that demanded capital ships have protection beneath the waterline. British dreadnoughts were designed with only a thin protective screen covering magazines and shell rooms and lacked adequate torpedo protection – a fact that helped shape the tactics at Jutland, where Admiral Jellico did not pursue the German Fleet at one point when it tried to make good its escape, fearing a torpedo boat destroyer attack on the precious warships of the Grand Fleet.

In contrast, the first German dreadnoughts were fitted with a continuous 1.25-inch anti-torpedo bulkhead that protected all vital below-deck spaces. In their second class of dreadnought, the British enhanced torpedo-protection by extending their protective screen over all the vital spaces, in the same fashion as the Germans. Later, British capital ships such as *Repulse* were fitted with anti-torpedo bulges, designed to detonate the torpedo as far as possible away from the ship's internal bulkheads and negate the blast. The bulge gave a high level of protection against the small torpedo warheads of the day.

Both the Royal Navy and the German Imperial Navy attempted to provide further torpedo protection with internal subdivision schemes, where spaces and compartments inside the hull and torpedo bulge were designed to withstand and negate any blast. The Germans here were more successful, as their ships had wider beams and closer sub-division requirements.

Propulsion

The Royal Navy introduced coal-fired turbines with *Dreadnought* in 1906 – a bold decision, but one that brought instant weight-savings of some 1,000 tons, compared to the older reciprocating machinery. That weight-saving could be used to provide additional armour or guns. The turbine also proved more reliable than the older machinery and allowed the new ships to steam at higher speeds for longer distances.

During World War I, the design of later capital ships featured the use of oil fuel instead of coal. The advantages of oil were obvious – when burned, oil provides 30% more heat per pound than coal, so the use of oil suspended the need to re-coal every few days. Oil required no stokers and emitted much less smoke than coal, which obscured gun laying and made the ships much more visible on the horizon. Refueling by oil was also much faster and easier, and beginning with the Queen Elizabeth class of super-dreadnoughts commissioned in 1915–16, all British dreadnoughts were oil-fired. The five Queen Elizabeth dreadnoughts were the fastest battleships of the day, with new propulsion systems and the inclusion of the 15-inch gun (instead of the 13.5-inch gun), along with increased armour. Additionally, because the weight of the 15-inch shell was so much greater than the 13.5-inch, designers were able to move to an eight-gun battery in four double turrets on the battleships, instead of the customary ten guns. This dispensed with the midships' Q turret and allowed the space gained to be devoted to propulsion.

Later developments

At the beginning of World War I, on 18 December 1914, Admiral Lord Fisher presented his requirements for a new breed of his battlecruiser concept to the Director of Naval Construction. He wanted new battlecruisers with a long, high, flared bow, like that on the old pre-dreadnought HMS *Renown*, with four 15-inch guns in two twin turrets, an anti-torpedo boat armament of twenty 4-inch guns mounted high up and protected by gun shields only, and 6-inch armour – as compared to battleship armour of 12–14 inches. He subsequently increased the number of 15-inch guns he required to six, and added a requirement for two torpedo tubes. Fisher believed that the next class of German battlecruiser would steam at 28 knots – so he demanded a speed of 32 knots for the new British ships. Compare this to the 23-knot speed of the battleship of the day.

The planned construction of two Royal Sovereign-class battleships had been approved, but they had not yet been laid down. The Director of Naval Construction, Eustace Tennyson d'Eyncourt, quickly produced an entirely new design of battlecruiser to meet Admiral Lord Fisher's requirements, and the builders agreed to deliver two of the new Renown-class battlecruisers in place of the two approved Royal Sovereign-class battleships, in 15 months. The new battlecruisers *Renown* and *Repulse* had been conceived – a radical, fast, new addition to the British Grand Fleet. These two brand new, state of the art 1916 Renown-class battlecruisers *Repulse* and *Renown* were fitted with the new bigger 15-inch guns, six of them set in three twin turrets. They also received the new oil-propulsion system. The weight savings on gun turret, armour and coal gave the Renown-class battlecruisers the top speed of 32 knots Fisher had demanded – fast even by today's standards – and allowing them to easily out run a battleship of the day.

At the end of World War I, all the battleships of the German High Seas Fleet were scuttled at Scapa Flow on 21 June 1919, and for many years Germany simply had no battleships. The period between the wars saw battleship construction subjected to international treaty limitations to prevent another costly arms race breaking out.

By the mid 1930s however, as the international situation started to deteriorate, Japan and Italy withdrew from the treaties, and Britain realised that it was badly short of modern battleships. The Royal Navy had long since stopped building battlecruisers. The Admiralty thus set in motion plans for the construction of a new class of fast battleship: the King George V class. The Royal Navy, United States Navy and Imperial Japanese Navy all extensively upgraded and modernised their World War I-era capital ships during the 1930s, with increased tower height and stability for rangefinding equipment, more armour against plunging fire and aerial bombing, and extra anti-aircraft weapons. Some British ships received a new block superstructure called 'Queen Anne's castle', and this would be used in the five new King George V fast battleships; the most modern British battleships used during World War II. The five new battleships were: *King George V* completed in 1940; *Prince of Wales* (1941); *Duke of York* (1941); *Howe* (1942); and *Anson* (1942).

The new class of King George V fast battleships could make 28 knots and were fitted with two quad 14-inch turrets, one fore and one aft, and a superfiring forward twin 14-inch B turret, situated behind and above the forward quad A turret. With the increased speed of the new breed of fast battleship, battleships could now achieve the best of both worlds – armour and speed.

As World War II unfolded, the new King George V-class battleships found themselves deployed alongside older pre-war battleships and refitted World War I-era battlecruisers such as *Repulse* and HMS *Hood*.

Naval tactics

In the battleship era, 'attack speed' or 'action speed' meant the same thing as 'full speed'. In the case of battleships, that was about 23 knots on the German side and 24 knots on the British side during World War I; and 28 knots during World War II. The two opposing sides would manoeuvre at full speed on the vast expanses of the open sea to try and secure the tactically most favourable position. Aside from the performance of the ship and its guns, which would be well known before combat, commanders also had to take account of a number of natural factors and apply fighting tactics to those factors to determine the value of a combat position.

(a) Nature

Commanders had to take account of local variables such as (a) the direction of the wind; (b) the sun's position; (c) sea conditions; and (d) visibility. They all had to be taken into account in determining how to fight.

Commanders would manoeuvre to avoid getting into a combat position where the smoke from their own guns hung in front of them or drifted towards the enemy line, as this would obscure vision, rangefinding and gun laying.

If an enemy ship had the sun behind it during the day, then it had an advantage, because gunnery officers trying to train the director on the enemy would be dazzled in much the same way as if you looked at the sun with binoculars. The silhouettes of hostile ships towards the sun would be far less sharp. At sunset, however, commanders would try to get into a position where they were hidden in the darkness of night whilst their enemy was silhouetted against the fading light of the setting sun in the west. If one side successfully got into a position with light and visibility in their favour, then they may be able to easily see the enemy ship whilst being concealed themselves from the enemy, as if shrouded in a cloak of invisibility.

It was also unfavourable if a battleship had to shoot towards a high rolling sea, as spray would often billow up over the guns and conning tower, making it difficult for the gunnery officer at the telescopic sight on the conning tower behind B turret, as well as for the gun crew.

(b) Fighting positions

Apart from these local tactical advantages of nature, there were other tactical fighting positions for the ships to try to achieve. If a ship had the enemy at right angles to her bows, the enemy could use all her main guns and half her secondary armament in a broadside, whilst the ship bow on could only fire from one or two forward turrets. The enemy had crossed the T of the ship bow on – a feared position to be in and one which commanders did their best to avoid. Whole squadrons or fleets would strive to achieve this classic naval manoeuvre of 'crossing the T', and it was the aim of the faster ships to get across the head of the enemy column in order to 'enfilade' it, that is, to get the enemy under fire from ahead and force it back.

If the leading ships of a fleet 'crossing the T' are well organized, the battle line of the whole fleet will gradually become circular, the circle getting smaller and smaller. This should only happen to an enemy fleet when it is surprised by the sudden appearance of opposing ships – and this is exactly what happened to the German line at the Battle of Jutland. Here, the main British Grand Fleet suddenly materialised in line astern from beneath the horizon in front of the vanguard of the German Fleet, as Beatty and his pulverized Battlecruiser Fleet fled north after the initial contact, all the time drawing the chasing German Fleet behind him to a pre-arranged rendezvous with the Grand Fleet coming down from Scapa Flow. As it appeared, the British Grand Fleet was stretched out along almost the whole horizon – all the British ships in range could fire broadsides with all their big guns at the lead ships of the German Fleet now racing towards them in line astern. Only the lead ships in the German vanguard could return fire with their two forward turrets. The classic naval manoeuvre had been achieved.

A fleet usually steamed in 'line ahead' or 'line astern', and usually the strongest squadron of battleships would be at the front in the vanguard and the weakest in the rear. The fast battlecruisers such as *Repulse* would usually take station ahead of the battleships and would also be in line ahead/astern. Ahead of the battlecruisers, the much quicker light cruisers would be disposed as a scouting force. The usual steaming speed of the fleet would be in the region of 15–17 knots, although when on active patrol, the ships would have steam up in the boilers so that they could put on full steam and get up to attack speed if the enemy were sighted.

CHAPTER TWO

HMS *PRINCE OF WALES* (BATTLESHIP 1939):

FROM BIRKENHEAD 1937 TO SINGAPORE 1941

The battleship HMS Prince of Wales. *(IWM)*

Construction & specifications

The Terms of the 1930 Treaty of London extended a ban on battleship construction introduced by the 1921 Five-Power Treaty – also known as the Washington Treaty. The second London Naval Treaty of 1936 set the displacement limit for future battleships at 35,000 tons and capped gun size at a maximum of 16 inches. Britain would comply with that treaty but Germany, who had also signed, was designing the Bismarck-class battleships *Bismarck* and *Tirpitz*, which would displace 41,700 long tons standard and almost 50,000 long tons at full load. Japan, who had refused to sign the treaty, would soon build their two Yamato-class super battleships, *Yamato* and *Musashi*, which each displaced almost 70,000 long tons standard (72,000 tons combat load) and were fitted with 18.1-inch guns.

With the coming to power of Hitler and the Nazis in 1933, the seemingly almost unbelievable possibility of another global conflict became a reality. By 1936, in the face of the growing Nazi threat, Britain had woken up to the fact that she was woefully short of modern battleships. The Admiralty thus set in motion plans for the construction of a new class of fast battleship – the King George V class. Because of the urgent need for battleships, the Admiralty did not have enough time to re-work their specifications to equip the new ships with a larger 16-inch main gun arrangement. They would be fitted with the tried-and-tested 14-inch main guns – an advanced design with a range of 36,000 yards (over 20 miles) – and a high rate of fire. Powerful and modern though they were, the King George V-class battleships were being built within the restrictive terms of the London Naval Treaties at a time when their enemy on the seas would be the far larger and more powerful German Bismarck- and Japanese Yamato-class battleships.

When she was conceived, HMS *Prince of Wales* was originally to have been named *King Edward VIII*, but the abdication of Edward VIII on 11 December 1936 forced a hurried change of name to *Prince of Wales* before construction started.

A month after the abdication, on 1 January 1937, *Prince of Wales* was laid down at Cammell Laird's shipyard in Birkenhead. Her construction took more than two years but she was finally launched before a crowd of 50,000 on 3 May 1939, just four months before World War II started. She was still being fitted out afloat when war was declared in September 1939 – the outbreak of hostilities and an urgent need for battleships caused her construction schedule (and that of her sister battleship *King George V*) to be accelerated. The late delivery of gun-mountings and some German bomb damage whilst she was in her fitting-out berth caused delays in her outfitting, but she was finally commissioned on 19 January 1941. The Admiralty chose Captain John C. Leach to command their new battleship, a talented officer who specialized in naval gunnery and had served in battleships in World War I and commanded the cruiser *Cumbria* before World War II.

Model showing the arrangement of the four propellers of HMS Prince of Wales

Anchor hawse pipes

Bow

Anchor capstans

Director Control Tower

Wash deflector

Dual purpose 5.25-inch turrets P3 & P4

Seaplane/boat crane

Dual purpose 5.25-inch turrets P1 & P2

"A" turret quadruple 14-inch guns

"B" turret twin 14-inch guns

Dual purpose 5.25-inch secondary armamanet turrets S1 & S2

Y turret twin 14-inch guns

Dual purpose 5.25-inch turrets S3 & S4

Seaplane catapult deck

Prince of Wales general deck layout

Prince of Wales was 745 ft 1 in. long overall, with a maximum beam of 112 ft 5 in. and a standard draft of 29 ft (35 ft 6 in. maximum). She displaced 36,727 long tons (37,300 tons) as standard and 43,786 long tons (44,500 tons) fully loaded for combat. She carried a crew of 1502 officers and men.

Prince of Wales was powered by Parsons-geared steam turbines, driving four propeller shafts. Steam was provided by eight Admiralty 3-drum water-tube boilers, which normally delivered 100,000 shaft horsepower (shp), but could deliver 110,000 shp at emergency overload, giving *Prince of Wales* a top speed of 28 knots.

The ship carried 3,542 long tons (3,600 tons) of fuel oil, and at full speed, *Prince of Wales* had a range of 3,100 nautical miles, with a range of 10,250 nautical miles at a cruising speed of 15 knots.

Prince of Wales was protected by a 14.7-inch-thick main vertical side armour belt which tapered down to 5.5 inches at its end and ran from forward of A turret to aft of Y turret. Armoured bulkheads ran athwartships, connecting each end of her side armour belts to form the armoured box, the citadel. The forward bulkhead was 11.7 inches thick, the aft bulkheads being 9.8 inches and 4 inches thick. Her main deck had 6-inch-thick armour over her magazines and her lower deck armour was 5 inches.

Prince of Wales was fitted with ten breach loading (B.L.)14-inch Mk VII guns, the turrets for which had 12.7-inch-thick armour on their sides, 6.9 inches at the rear and 5.9 inches on the roof. The walls of the barbettes (the armoured cylinders that housed the ammunition hoists and turning apparatus for the turrets and ran down to the magazines in the bowels of the ship) were up to 16 inches thick.

The 14-inch guns were mounted, four in one quadruple turret forward (A turret), with a superfiring twin-barreled turret (B turret) behind it. A further quadruple 14-inch Y turret was set aft. The guns could be elevated 40 degrees and depressed 3 degrees by hydraulic drives, with rates of 2 and 8 degrees per second respectively. A salvo could be fired every 40 seconds.

The secondary armament consisted of 16 dual-purpose Quick Firing (QF) 5.25-inch Mk I guns which were mounted in eight twin mounts, four either side, and which could elevate to 70 degrees and depress 5 degrees. The maximum range of these 5.25-inch guns was 24,070 yards at a 45-degree elevation and the upper limit for anti-aircraft use was 49,000 feet. The design rate of fire was 10–12 rounds per minute – although seven to eight rounds per minute was more average.

Along with her main and secondary batteries, *Prince of Wales* carried six eight-barreled quick-firing 2-pounder Vickers 'Pom-Pom' anti-aircraft guns – so called due to the sound the earlier models made when firing. These multiple 40mm gun mounts required four different types of gun and were nicknamed the 'Chicago Piano'. The mount had two rows of four guns, which were produced in both right hand and left hand and inner and outer, so that the feed and ejector mechanisms matched. She also carried 40mm Bofors anti-aircraft autocannon, a number of Oerlikon light cannons, Lewis machine guns and 80 UP (unrotated projectile) – a short-range rocket-firing anti-aircraft weapon used extensively in the early days of World War II by the Royal Navy.

World War II

Bismarck action

During early August 1940, while she was still being outfitted in Cammell Laird's Birkenhead Shipyard, German aircraft attacked *Prince of Wales*. One bomb fell between the ship and a wet basin wall, narrowly missing a 100-ton dockside crane, and exploded underwater below the bilge keel. The explosion took place about six feet from the ship's port side in the vicinity of the after group of 5.25-inch guns. Hull plating for 20–30 feet was buckled and rivets were sprung. Significant flooding occurred in the port outboard compartments in the area of damage, bringing on a 10-degree port list. The flooding was made worse because final compartment air tests had not yet been made and the ship did not have her pumping-system in operation.

A local fire company and the shipyard pumped the water out, and *Prince of Wales* was thereafter dry-docked for permanent repairs. This bomb damage and the delay in delivery of her main guns and turrets delayed her completion throughout the rest of 1939 and 1940, as Britain fought for survival.

As the early part of the war progressed – unfavourably for Britain – the need for capital ships became urgent. In September 1939, the old battleship *Royal Oak* was torpedoed and sunk at Scapa Flow and the aircraft carrier *Courageous* was torpedoed off Ireland by *U-29*. In June 1940, the British aircraft carrier *Glorious* and her two escort destroyers were caught off Norway and sunk by the German battlecruisers *Scharnhorst* and *Gneisenau*. During the summer and autumn of 1940, the Battle of Britain developed – the largest and most sustained aerial bombing campaign to that date. From July onwards, coastal shipping convoys and shipping centres such as Portsmouth were targeted. The *Luftwaffe* shifted its focus to RAF airfields and infrastructure one month later, before moving to terror-bombing tactics on British towns and cities. In the face of such demands on land and at sea, completion of *Prince of Wales* was advanced by postponing compartment air tests, ventilation tests and full testing of her bilge, ballast and fuel oil systems. She was rushed into service and commissioned on 19 January 1941, although she was far from battle-ready at that time.

A few months later on 22 May 1941, after training exercises at Scapa Flow, *Prince of Wales*, the World War I era battlecruiser *Hood* and six destroyers were ordered to take station south of Iceland and intercept the German battleship *Bismarck* if she attempted to break out into the Atlantic. Captain Leach knew that breakdowns with the big guns were likely to occur, since Vickers Armstrong technicians had already had to deal with failures that had taken place during the recent Scapa Flow training exercises. Captain Leach personally requested that these technicians remained aboard. They did so and played an important role in the ensuing action.

On 23 May, *Bismarck*, in company with the heavy cruiser *Prinz Eugen* and three destroyers, was reported to have left Bergen, heading south-west in the Denmark Strait. She had not replenished her fuel stores while she was previously stationed at Gotenhafen and had been some 200 tons short of a full fuel load when she left for Bergen. The voyage to Bergen had used up a further 1000 tons of fuel.

At 7.22 p.m., using hydrophone and radar, the German flotilla detected the patrolling 10,000-ton County-class heavy cruiser HMS *Suffolk*, and the German ships knew that their

Port beam view of HMS Prince of Wales

location had been reported. *Prinz Eugen* turned to attack *Suffolk*, which retreated to a safe distance and continued to shadow the German flotilla.

At 8 p.m., Vice-Admiral Lancelot Holland in *Hood*, the flagship of the force stationed south of Iceland, ordered the squadron to steam at 27 knots to the reported location of the powerful German group to reinforce *Suffolk* and the other County-class heavy cruiser *Norfolk* (still patrolling the Denmark Strait) and to engage the German raiders. The rest of the Home Fleet at Scapa Flow was placed on high alert and 18 bombers were scrambled to attack the German flotilla, but were ultimately unable to locate the German ships due to bad weather and low cloud.

At 8.30 p.m., the other patrolling cruiser, HMS *Norfolk* rendezvoused with *Suffolk* and together the two cruisers shadowed the German ships throughout the night. The Battle of the Denmark Strait had unknowingly just begun.

In the dark of the wee small hours of 24 May, at 2 a.m., the fast destroyers of the onrushing main British force were sent out as a screen to search for the German ships to the north. At 2.47 a.m., *Hood* and *Prince of Wales* increased speed to 28 knots and changed course slightly to obtain a better angle of approach to the German ships. The weather improved with 10-mile visibility and by 5.10 a.m., both crews were at action stations.

At 5.37 a.m., look-outs on *Prince of Wales* spotted the German ships about 17 nautical miles away, and course was changed to starboard to close the range. *Hood*, although a world-known and revered battlecruiser, was by now 25 years old and was lightly armoured in comparison to a battleship. In particular, dating back to World War I, when ranges and elevations of guns were lower, she lacked adequate horizontal deck armour against plunging fire from modern big guns firing over great distances at high elevation. Whilst her side armour belt ranged from 6–12 inches thick, her horizontal deck armour was only 0.75–3-inches thick. As a result, her commander knew that she would have to close the range quickly – by so doing she would become progressively less vulnerable to plunging shellfire at shorter ranges when her side armour would take the enemy shell hits.

As a modern, state-of-the-art battleship, *Prince of Wales* had far thicker vertical side armour of 5.4–14.7 inches, and with deck armour of 5–6 inches she was far less vulnerable to plunging fire from enemy big guns.

The original British battle plan had been for *Prince of Wales* and *Hood* to concentrate on

Bismarck, while the cruisers *Norfolk* and *Suffolk* were to engage *Prinz Eugen*. The Royal Navy had intended to contact the German vessels at 2 a.m., when *Bismarck* and *Prinz Eugen* would be silhouetted against the sun's afterglow (sunset at this latitude was 1.51 a.m.). This would allow the British ships to approach rapidly and unseen in darkness to a range close enough not to endanger *Hood* from plunging fire from *Bismarck*.

The plan's success depended on *Suffolk* maintaining unbroken contact with the German ships – but *Suffolk* lost contact with *Bismarck* for a period during the night. Contact was regained just before 3 a.m., when *Hood* and *Prince of Wales* were about 35 nautical miles away. The loss of contact now put the British ships at a disadvantage, as the ships would converge at a wider angle – much more slowly than in a swift head on approach. *Hood* would be left exposed to *Bismarck*'s plunging fire for a much longer period.

As the ships closed, *Prince of Wales* opened fire on *Bismarck* at 20,000 yards. *Hood* opened fire at 5.52 a.m., at a distance of 26,500 yards, firing initially at *Prinz Eugen*. *Hood*'s first salvo straddled *Prinz Eugen*, but in less than three minutes, at 5.55 a.m., she herself was struck by 8-inch shells from *Prinz Eugen*.

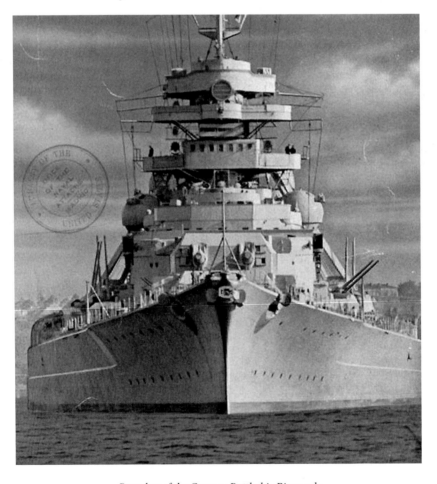

Bow shot of the German Battleship Bismarck

The heavy cruiser HMS Suffolk *played a crucial role shadowing* Bismarck *during the opening stages of the Battle of the Denmark Strait*

The first shots by *Prince of Wales* at *Bismarck* – two salvoes of 14-inch shells – were 1,000 yards over. The turret rangefinders on *Prince of Wales* could not be used because of spray over the bow from the heavy seas, and fire was instead directed from the 15-foot (4.6-m) rangefinders in the control tower.

The approach of the British ships was now too fine – and with the German ships only 30 degrees on the starboard bow, the British aft turrets could not be brought to bear to fire. *Prinz Eugen*, with *Bismarck* astern, had the *Prince of Wales* and *Hood* slightly forward of the beam and both ships could deliver full broadsides with all their big guns.

The third salvo from *Prince of Wales* straddled *Bismarck*. She went on to score three hits in total on *Bismarck* – with two of the hits being decisive. One shell holed her bow and the other shell struck *Bismarck*'s hull underwater below her side armour belt and exploded inside the ship. Consequent flooding of the auxiliary boiler machinery room forced the shutdown of two boilers due to a slow leak in the boiler room immediately aft. The damage to her bow cut off access to the forward tanks holding 1,000 tons of fuel oil and caused a trailing slick of oil. *Bismarck*'s speed dropped by 2 knots and she took on a 9-degree list to port and settled down at her bow by 2 metres. The losses of fuel and boiler power were decisive factors in the *Bismarck*'s subsequent decision to return to port in France for repair.

'A' turret of *Prince of Wales* went out of action after the first salvo, due to a defect. Fire continued with the remaining guns, but sporadic breakdowns continued to occur as the action progressed.

At 5.57 a.m., at a range of 16,500 yards, Vice-Admiral Holland ordered his force to turn to port to open the range and allow the main guns on both ships to be trained on *Bismarck*. As that turn was being executed, at 6.01 a.m., a salvo from *Bismarck* straddled *Hood* abreast her mainmast. Those on *Prince of Wales* saw a huge pillar of orange flame that shot upwards, followed by an explosion that destroyed a large portion of the ship from midships to the rear of Y turret. The ship broke in two, the stern sinking quickly. The bow rose to point upwards before sinking beneath the sea.

1,415 men had just lost their lives, with only three of her crew surviving.

Prince of Wales had fired at *Bismarck* unopposed until, on Holland's order, she began her port turn at 5.57 a.m., when *Prinz Eugen* began to target her. After *Hood* exploded at 6.01 a.m., the German ships were able to concentrate their fire on *Prince of Wales*, with a combination of their 15-inch, 8-inch, and 5.9-inch guns.

In all, *Prince of Wales* was struck by some four shots from *Bismarck* and three shells from *Prinz Eugen*. One heavy blow struck her below the waterline as she manouevered through the wreckage of *Hood*. Another 15-inch shell struck the starboard side of her compass platform and killed the majority of the personnel there. The navigating officer was wounded, but Captain Leach was unhurt. Pieces of another shell struck her radar office aft, killing the crew there. An 8-inch shell from *Prinz Eugen* penetrated to the propelling-charge and round-manipulation chamber below the aft 5.25-inch gun turrets. A 15-inch shell also penetrated the ship's side below the armour belt amidships but failed to explode, coming to rest in the wing compartments on the starboard side of the after boiler rooms. The shell was discovered and defused when the ship was later docked at Rosyth.

At 6.05 a.m., faced with this onslaught and serious gunnery malfunctions (that now left only two of the ship's ten main 14-inch guns still able to fire) and the damage to his ship, Captain Leach decided to disengage and re-engage at a more favourable opportunity.

Prince of Wales laid down a heavy smokescreen to cover her escape. As she withdrew, she fired from her rear turret, under local control at the turret until the turret suffered a jammed shell ring, which cut off the ammunition supply and made her big 14-inch quad guns inoperable. It took until 8.25 a.m. for technicians to repair the shell ring and get the four big guns of Y turret back into action. *Prince of Wales* radioed the *Norfolk* to advise that *Hood* had been sunk and then steamed to join *Norfolk* and *Suffolk* on station some 15 to 17 miles astern of *Bismarck*. Thirteen of her crew were dead and nine wounded.

The Bismarck, *well down by the head following the hit from* Prince of Wales, *runs for repair in France as the Royal Navy closes in*

At 8.01 a.m., *Bismarck* turned to head towards St Nazaire in France for repairs, trailing broad streams of oil on both sides of her wake. All Royal Navy warships in the vicinity were tasked to join the pursuit of *Bismarck* and *Prinz Eugen* as they ran at speed back to France. The light cruisers *Manchester*, *Birmingham* and *Arethusa* were ordered to patrol the Denmark Strait to detect and interdict any attempt by the German raiders to retrace their steps to Bergen. The battleship *Rodney*, which had been escorting RMS *Britannic* to Boston, joined the British group and two old Revenge-class battleships:

Revenge (from Halifax) and *Ramillies*; which had been on convoy escort duty, were also detached.

In total, six battleships and battlecruisers (including *Repulse*), two aircraft carriers, 13 cruisers and 21 destroyers were committed to the chase.

By 5 p.m., the crew on *Prince of Wales* had restored nine of her ten main 14-inch guns to service and she was put to the vanguard of the small formation of three British ships (with *Norfolk* and *Suffolk*) shadowing the two German raiders.

At 6.14 p.m., *Prinz Eugen* detached from *Bismarck*, and *Bismarck* came about to face her pursuers. *Suffolk* was forced to turn away at high speed at this unexpected manoeuvre. *Prince of Wales* fired 12 salvoes at *Bismarck*, which in turn responded with nine salvoes, none of which struck. The action had, however, successfully diverted British attention from *Prinz Eugen*, which had managed to slip away. *Bismarck* resumed her heading to St Nazaire, with *Suffolk*, *Norfolk* and *Prince of Wales* shadowing her on her port side.

Although *Bismarck* had been damaged and her speed reduced, she could still make 28 knots – the same as the top speed of the undamaged battleship *King George V*, which had also been ordered into the fray, with her powerful 14-inch guns. Unless *Bismarck* could be further slowed down, the British battleships and aircraft carriers would not be able to catch her before she reached St Nazaire.

At 4 p.m., the aircraft carrier *Victorious* (and four light cruisers) were detached to a course that would allow her to attack with her torpedo-bombers – and at 10 p.m., a carrier aircraft strike was launched. Nine antiquated Fairey Swordfish torpedo-bombers attacked, supported by six Fairey Fulmar fighters. After nearly attacking *Norfolk* by mistake, the attack went in on *Bismarck*. *Bismarck* evaded eight of the torpedoes but the ninth torpedo struck amidships on the armour belt, causing little damage.

Although the torpedo had caused insignificant damage, the rapid and violent changes of speed and course by *Bismarck* as she manouevered to avoid torpedoes, had loosened collision mats, which had been plugging the hole in her hull caused by a shell from *Prince of Wales*. As a result, flooding through the forward shell hole increased and port-side No 2 boiler room had to be abandoned. Two boilers serving the port shaft were now out of action. Coupled with decreasing fuel levels and an increasing bow trim from flooding, *Bismarck* slowed to 16 knots.

Ship's divers were able to repair the collision mats in the bow, and once done, *Bismarck* was able to increase her speed to 20 knots – which her officers calculated was the most economical speed for the voyage to France in light of her low fuel stores. *Prince of Wales* and *Bismarck* had one other brief skirmish with neither ship scoring any hits. *Bismarck* again had to slow her speed, to 12 knots, to allow divers to connect hoses and pump fuel from the forward compartments to the rear tanks.

The British ships were zigzagging every ten minutes to avoid any U-boats that may have been sent to assist *Bismarck*. The Germans were monitoring the regular British zigzagging, and at one point during the night, at 3 a.m., when the British ships were at the extremity of a zigzag and out of radar range, the German commander Lütjens turned *Bismarck* to the west and then to the north doubling back on his pursuers and coming up behind them. The three British ships searched for her without success, the search becoming frantic as they were now also running low on fuel.

British code-breakers ashore managed to decrypt some German signals, which included an order for Lütjens to head for Brest, with *Luftwaffe* units to redeploy there to assist her. When French Resistance fighters confirmed the movement of *Luftwaffe* aircraft, British naval forces were turned towards France and concentrated in the areas where it was believed *Bismarck* would pass.

A squadron of PBY Catalina aircraft from Northern Ireland joined the search and at 10.30 a.m. on 26 May, *Bismarck* was spotted 690 nautical northwest of Brest by one of the Catalina planes. Ominously, it was calculated that at her then speed, she would reach the protection of the U-boats and *Luftwaffe* in less than a day – quicker than any British forces could catch her.

Force H, centered on the aircraft carrier *Ark Royal*, was already steaming north to the area from Gibraltar. To the north, the carrier *Victorious*, along with *Prince of Wales*, *Suffolk* and *Repulse*, were all forced to break off the search due to fuel concerns. The only heavy Royal Navy ships remaining in the chase were *King George V* and *Rodney* – but they were too far away to successfully intercept in time.

Ark Royal's Swordfish torpedo-bombers were also in the air, searching unarmed, when the Catalina planes from Northern Ireland located *Bismarck*. Several torpedo-bombers also confirmed *Bismarck*'s location – only 60nm away from *Ark Royal*. The torpedo-bombers were immediately ordered to return to *Ark Royal*, arm with magnetic torpedoes and prepare for an attack.

Once armed, the Swordfish took off, and in a case of mistaken identity in poor conditions, accidentally attacked HMS *Sheffield*. Luckily, the magnetic detonators failed to work properly and no significant damage was caused to *Sheffield* by the impacts. The Swordfish returned to *Ark Royal*, where they were re-armed with more reliable contact detonators on the torpedoes.

At 7.10 p.m., 15 aircraft launched from *Ark Royal* for a second attack, and at 8.47 p.m., they began their attack descent through clouds towards *Bismarck*. She immediately opened fire and began to turn violently to allow her anti-aircraft batteries to fire at the slow incoming bombers.

Bismarck avoided all bar two of the torpedoes. One hit amidships on her port side, just below the bottom edge of the main armour belt. The force of the explosion was largely contained by the underwater protection system and armour belt, but some minor flooding did occur. The second torpedo struck *Bismarck* on the port side at her stern, beside the port rudder shaft. The coupling on the port rudder assembly was badly damaged and the rudder could not be disengaged – it was locked in a 12-degree turn to port. Attempts by the crew to restore steering managed to repair the starboard rudder, but the port rudder was badly jammed and could not be freed. Blowing the rudder off with explosives was considered, but it was felt that it would cause too much damage to the nearby propellers.

At 9.15 p.m., Lütjens reported that the ship was unmanoeuvrable. With the port rudder jammed, *Bismarck* was now steering in a large circle. This gave the necessary time for the distant British heavy forces to close. The battleships *King George V* and *Rodney* now raced to intercept *Bismarck*, along with the heavy cruisers *Dorsetshire* and *Norfolk*.

At 9.40 p.m., fully aware of the fate that awaited his ship, Lütjens signalled headquarters: 'Ship unmanoeuvrable. We will fight to the last shell. Long live the *Führer*'.

British light forces harassed the beleaguered German battleship throughout the night and into the next morning, as the heavy British battleships and carrier raced towards her for the kill.

After daybreak on 27 May, *King George V* arrived on the scene to lead the attack, followed by *Rodney* on her port quarter. At a range of 25,000 yards, *Rodney* opened up first with her two forward 16-inch turrets – a total of six big guns. *King George V* then opened up with her

14-inch guns. As the British forces closed, *Norfolk* and *Dorsetshire* were able to begin firing with their 8-inch guns.

At 9.02 a.m., a 16-inch shell from *Rodney* struck *Bismarck*'s forward superstructure, killing hundreds of men and damaging and disabling the two forward turrets which were only able to fire one last salvo at 9.27 a.m. before falling silent.

The main gunnery control station on *Bismarck* was quickly destroyed and the rear control station took over firing control for the still-functioning rear turrets. Three salvoes were successfully fired – but then a British shell destroyed the gun director. With coordinated gunnery control disabled, an order was given for the remaining guns to fire independently. By 9.31 a.m., all four main battery turrets were out of action.

By 10 a.m., the two British battleships had fired over 700 main battery shells and *Bismarck* was aflame from stem to stern. She had taken on a list of 20 degrees to port and was low in the water by the stern. *Rodney* closed to point-blank range of 3,000 yards and continued firing into the stricken German battleship – the Royal Navy vessels could not cease firing until the Germans lowered their battle ensigns or abandoned ship. They did neither.

At 10.20 a.m., *Dorsetshire* closed and fired torpedoes into *Bismarck*'s raised starboard side. *Dorsetshire* then moved to *Bismarck*'s port side and fired another torpedo. Around 10.35 a.m., the port list worsened suddenly. *Bismarck* capsized and started to sink slowly by the stern. She disappeared at 10.40 a.m., leaving hundreds of German sailors struggling for their lives in the water.

Dorsetshire and the destroyer *Maori* closed and lowered ropes to pull in survivors, but at 11.40 a.m., reports arrived that a U-boat had been spotted in the area. Experience had already shown that U-boats would attack and sink vessels stopped in the water to rescue survivors of sinkings. These stationery and valuable British warships could not be put at risk. The British ships abandoned the rescue effort, with *Dorsetshire* having picked up 85 men and *Maori* 25 men.

The Atlantic Charter

Following repairs of her battle scars at Rosyth, *Prince of Wales* was selected to take Prime Minister Winston Churchill across the Atlantic to Newfoundland for a conference with US President Franklin D. Roosevelt. She arrived there on 9 August 1941, escorted by the destroyers HMS *Ripley,* HMCS *Assiniboine* and HMCS *Restigouche*. At Placentia Bay, Newfoundland, Roosevelt transferred to the destroyer USS *McDougal* and came out to meet Winston Churchill aboard *Prince of Wales*. At the end of the conference, the Atlantic Charter was proclaimed, which set out Allied goals for a post-war world. Following the signing of the charter, *Prince of Wales* re-crossed the Atlantic, arriving back at Scapa Flow on 18 August 1941.

A religious service takes place aboard HMS Prince of Wales during the Atlantic Charter Conference

The leaders of America and Britain meet aboard HMS Prince of Wales *during the Atlantic Charter Conference*

The USS McDougal *alongside HMS* Prince of Wales *for the Atlantic Charter Conference*

Force H – the Mediterranean

In September 1941, *Prince of Wales* was assigned to Force H in the Mediterranean, forming part of Group II, which consisted of the battleships *Prince of Wales* and *Rodney*, the cruisers *Kenya*, *Edinburgh*, *Sheffield*, and *Euryalus*, and twelve destroyers. Force H provided the escort for Operation Halberd: a supply convoy from Gibraltar to Malta. On 27 September, Italian aircraft attacked the convoy and *Prince of Wales* shot down several aircraft with her 5.25-inch guns.

Later that day, there were reports that units of the Italian Fleet were approaching the convoy. *Prince of Wales*, *Rodney*, and the aircraft carrier *Ark Royal* were despatched to intercept, but the search proved fruitless. The convoy arrived in Malta without further incident and *Prince of Wales* returned to Gibraltar, before sailing on to the Royal Navy base at Scapa Flow, in the Orkney Islands of north Scotland. She arrived at the great 12-mile wide anchorage of Scapa Flow on 6 October 1941.

Force G – Singapore-bound

On 20 October 1941, the decision was made to send a small but powerful naval force to Singapore to deter Japanese aggression in the region. The backbone of the new squadron, now designated Force G, would be one of the new fast King George V-class battleships, and the old but fast World War I-era reconstructed battlecruiser HMS *Repulse* would be the second capital ship of the squadron. *Prince of Wales,* veteran of the *Bismarck* action and freshly returned from her convoy escort operations in the Mediterranean, was still at Scapa Flow. She was selected for the role and Captain Leach was summoned from Scapa Flow and given his preliminary orders for the battleship. The next two and a half days were spent filling the ship with ammunition, water, fuel and stores for the long voyage to the Far East.

At dawn on Thursday 23 October 1941, *Prince of Wales* and her two escort destroyers *Electra* and *Express* sailed out of Scapa Flow for Greenock, where the 53-year-old Admiral Sir Tom Phillips, who would command Force G, would come aboard. On reaching Greenock the following day, *Prince of Wales* moored out in the River whilst a succession of ships topped her up with oil, water and stores. Admiral Phillips and his staff came aboard and the Admiral's flag was hoisted on the new flagship.

Prince of Wales, now flagship of Force G, left Greenock on Saturday 25 October 1941, bound for Singapore via Freetown, Sierra Leone and Cape Town, escorted by the destroyers HMS *Electra*, HMS *Express*, and HMS *Hesperus*. Force G rendezvoused with HMS *Repulse* from the Indian Ocean at Colombo, Ceylon in November and proceeded to Singapore.

Force G arrived at Singapore and sailed round the island in a deliberate show of force before entering the naval dockyard to a tumultuous welcome on 2 December 1941. Just five days later on 7 December 1941, Japanese aircraft launched their surprise morning strike against the US Naval base at Hawaii. On 8 December, Japanese aircraft bombed Singapore.

CHAPTER THREE

HMS *REPULSE* (BATTLECRUISER 1916):

FROM CLYDEBANK 1915 TO SINGAPORE 1941

The battlecruiser HMS Repulse

Construction & specifications

Repulse was laid down on 25 January 1915, at John Brown's shipbuilding yard at Clydebank on the Clyde. Her sister ship *Renown* was laid down at nearby Fairfield's yard at Govan on the same day. *Repulse* was launched on 8 January 1916 and commissioned on 18 August 1916 – just a few months after the frailties of battlecruisers like her had been brutally exposed at the Battle of Jutland in May 1916. *Repulse* and her sister ship *Renown* were the world's fastest capital ships upon completion. Her construction had cost £2,829,087.

At the time of her construction in 1916, *Repulse* had an overall length of 794 ft 2.5 in., a beam of 89 ft 11.5 in., and a maximum draft of 29 ft 9 in. She displaced 26,854 long tons

(27,285 tons) at normal load and 31,592 long tons (32,099 tons) when fully loaded for combat.

The ship normally carried 1,000 long tons (1,016 tons) of fuel oil, but had a maximum capacity of 4,289 long tons (4,358 tons). With tanks full, she had a range at 18 knots of about 4,000 nautical miles (7,410 km). At the time of her launch she carried a crew of 1222.

Repulse was fitted with a main armament of six breach-loading (BL) 15-inch Mk I guns set in three twin hydraulically-driven gun turrets, designated 'A', 'B', and 'Y' from front to rear.

Her secondary armament consisted of seventeen 4-inch Mark VII guns, fitted in five triple and two single mounts. *Repulse* also carried a pair of 3-inch 20-cwt anti-aircraft guns mounted on the shelter deck abreast the rear funnel. She was fitted with two submerged 21-inch torpedo tubes, one on each side forward of 'A' barbette.

Repulse's waterline main armour belt of Krupp armour was 6 inches thick amidships. Her gun turrets had 7–9-inch-thick side armour with the turret roofs being 4.25 inches thick. Her high-tensile steel decks were designed initially from 0.75–1.5 inches in thickness, but after the frailties of the thin battlecruiser deck armour had been so tragically exposed at the Battle of Jutland in 1916, whilst *Repulse* was still being completed, an extra inch of high-tensile steel was added on the main deck over the magazines.

Repulse was fitted with a shallow anti-torpedo bulge along either side of her hull and integral to it. This air-filled bulge was intended to explode any torpedo before it hit the inner hull proper, and vent the underwater explosion to the surface rather than into the ship.

Repulse was the first capital ship fitted with a flying-off platform when an experimental platform was fitted on the roof of B turret in the autumn of 1917. Squadron Leader Rutland took off in a Sopwith Pup on 1 October. Another platform was built on Y turret and Rutland successfully took off from it on 8 October. One fighter and a reconnaissance aircraft were normally carried.

The 15-inch guns of A & B turrets on HMS Repulse, with the revolving top of the director control tower immediately aft and above the roof of B turret

World War I era

No 1 Battlecruiser Squadron and the Second Battle of Heligoland Bight

Repulse joined the Battlecruiser Force as flagship of No 1 Battlecruiser Squadron on 16 September 1916 and went on to participate in the Second Battle of Heligoland Bight in 1917. Here, along with the battlecruisers HMS *Courageous* and HMS *Glorious*, and the light cruisers *Calypso* and *Caledon*, she engaged the German battleships *Kaiser* and *Kaiserin*. This was the only heavy ship combat contact she saw during World War I.

Over the course of 1917 and in the lead up to that battle, the Admiralty had become concerned about German efforts in the North Sea to sweep paths through the British-laid minefields which were restricting the movements of the German High Seas Fleet and U-boats. A preliminary Royal Navy raid on German minesweepers on 31 October by light British vessels destroyed ten small German ships. The Admiralty then decided on a larger operation to destroy the minesweepers and their escorting light cruisers. Based on intelligence reports of German minesweeping operations, the Admiralty tasked two light cruiser squadrons and the 1st Cruiser Squadron to the operation. This naval force would be reinforced by 1st Battlecruiser Squadron, of which *Repulse* was part, and more distantly, by the battleships of the 1st Battle Squadron.

At 7.30 a.m., on 17 November 1917, silhouetted by the rising sun, the British force spotted four German light cruisers, eight destroyers, three divisions of minesweepers, eight *sperrbrecher* (cork-filled trawlers, used to detonate mines without sinking), and two trawlers used to mark the swept route. The British battlecruiser *Courageous* and the light cruiser *Cardiff* opened fire with their forward guns seven minutes later. The Germans responded by laying a thick smoke screen.

The British ships continued their attack but lost track of most of the smaller ships in the smoke, so concentrated fire on the German light cruisers as opportunity permitted. *Repulse* was detached not long after and raced forward at full speed to engage the enemy ships. She opened fire at about 9.00 a.m., and scored a single hit on the light cruiser SMS *Königsberg* during the battle, temporarily reducing her speed.

The German battleships SMS *Kaiser* and SMS *Kaiserin* were spotted about 9.50 a.m., and their presence forced the British to break off their pursuit. *Repulse* covered their retreat, aided by a heavy fog. *Repulse* had fired a total of 54 15-inch shells during the battle and scored the one confirmed hit on the light cruiser SMS *Königsberg*.

As a condition of the Armistice of 11 November 1918 – which suspended the hostilities of World War I pending the negotiation of the Treaty of Versailles – the 74 warships of the German Imperial Navy's High Seas Fleet were to be interned under British guard at Scapa Flow. The High Seas Fleet had survived the war relatively intact and could still pose a very real threat to the Allies if the Armistice broke down and the fighting restarted. Therefore, as a condition of the Armistice, the German Fleet would be interned at Scapa Flow under the close guard of the British. The High Seas Fleet was effectively to be held hostage during the peace negotiations. The First Battle Squadron of the British Grand Fleet – commanded by Sir Sydney Fremantle and consisting of five battleships, two light cruisers and nine destroyers – was stationed at Scapa Flow and would keep a watchful eye on the Germans.

The 74 ships of the German Fleet consisted of five massive battlecruisers, 11 battleships, eight cruisers and 50 torpedo-boat destroyers.

After crossing from their German bases, the High Seas Fleet rendezvoused with the entire British Grand Fleet at a pre-arranged location in the North Sea. *Repulse* was part of the British force. There were a combined 90,000 men afloat on 370 warships – no such massive sea force had ever been assembled before. The German warships had been ordered to have their guns disarmed before they left Germany and should have no longer been a threat to the British vessels, but the British were taking no chances of any German treachery: their guns were loaded and the crews at action-stations alertly looking for any signs of trouble.

The British Fleet split into two lines of battleships and battlecruisers, 6 miles apart and stretching out of sight into the distance. The German Fleet sailed into the middle of this passage of steel in single column and was escorted to Scapa Flow.

Inter-war years

A month after escorting the German Fleet into internment, *Repulse* began a major refit at Portsmouth on 17 December 1918 – intended to drastically improve her armour protection, as it was felt that despite the addition of extra armour whilst she was being completed in 1916, she was still too vulnerable to plunging fire. Her existing 6-inch armour belt was replaced by 9-inch armour plates, made surplus by the conversion of the battleship *Almirante Cochrane* (originally ordered by Chile and purchased after the war began) into the aircraft carrier HMS *Eagle*. The old 6-inch armour was fitted between the main and upper decks, above the new armour belt. Additional high-tensile plating was added to the decks over the magazines and steering gear. The ship's anti-torpedo bulge was deepened and reworked along the lines of that installed on the battleship HMS *Ramillies*, to cover her hull from the submerged torpedo room forward of A turret to 'Y' magazine, the inner compartments of the bulge being filled with crushing tubes. The bulges added 12 ft 8 in. to her beam and 1 ft 4 in. to her draft. Both flying-off platforms were removed. The refit increased her displacement by 4,500 long tons. Three 30-foot rangefinders were also added, along with eight torpedo tubes in twin-mounts on the upper deck.

Repulse was recommissioned on 1 January 1921, and joined the Battlecruiser Squadron of the Atlantic Fleet. In November 1923, the battlecruisers *Hood* and *Repulse* along with five light cruisers from the 1st Light Cruiser Squadron set out on a world cruise from west to east via the Panama Canal. They returned home ten months later in September 1924 after calling at ports in Africa, the Indian Ocean, the Far East, Australia, New Zealand, the Pacific, Canada and the USA.

Shortly after her return, the ship's pair of 3-inch anti-aircraft guns and her two single 4-inch gun mounts were removed and replaced with four Quick Firing (QF) 4-inch Mark V anti-aircraft guns. The Battlecruiser Squadron visited Lisbon in February 1925 to participate in the Vasco da Gama celebrations, before continuing on to the Mediterranean for exercises.

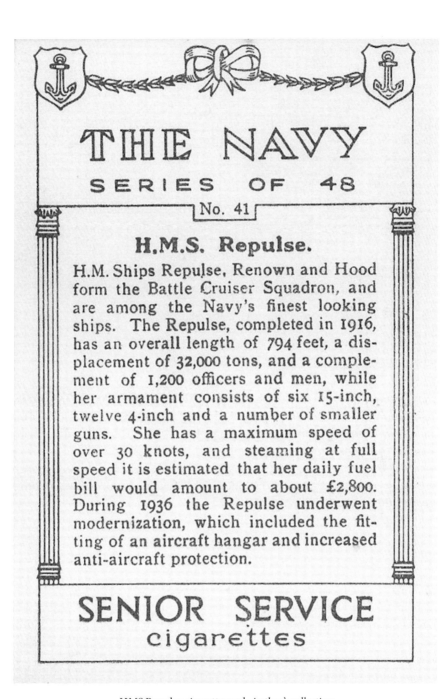

THE NAVY
SERIES OF 48
No. 41

H.M.S. Repulse.

H.M. Ships Repulse, Renown and Hood form the Battle Cruiser Squadron, and are among the Navy's finest looking ships. The Repulse, completed in 1916, has an overall length of 794 feet, a displacement of 32,000 tons, and a complement of 1,200 officers and men, while her armament consists of six 15-inch, twelve 4-inch and a number of smaller guns. She has a maximum speed of over 30 knots, and steaming at full speed it is estimated that her daily fuel bill would amount to about £2,800. During 1936 the Repulse underwent modernization, which included the fitting of an aircraft hangar and increased anti-aircraft protection.

SENIOR SERVICE
cigarettes

HMS Repulse *cigarette card. Author's collection*

Early postcard of HMS Repulse. *Author's collection*

1930s reconstruction

After *Repulse* completed her 1926 refit she remained in commission (aside from a brief refit in July–September 1927) with the Battlecruiser Squadron of the Atlantic Fleet until she was paid off in June 1932. She began a full reconstruction in April 1933, during which she was virtually rebuilt as part of the Royal Navy's modernisation.

Most of the existing layers of high-tensile steel that constituted the ship's horizontal deck armour were replaced by non-cemented armour plates 2.5–3.5 inches in thickness, and the torpedo control tower was removed from the aft superstructure. A fixed catapult replaced the midships 4-inch triple mount gun platform, and a hangar with an electric crane above it was built on each side of the rear funnel to house two of the ship's Fairey III seaplanes. One additional aircraft could be carried on the deck and another on the catapult itself.

The four 4-inch anti-aircraft guns were moved and set one pair abreast the rear funnel at the level of the hangar roof and the other pair abreast the fore funnel. Four prototype QF 4-inch Mark XV dual-purpose guns (surface and anti-aircraft) with a design range of 16,300 yards and an AA ceiling of 28,750 feet were added in twin mounts abreast the mainmast. Two 8-barreled Mark VI 2-pounder 'Pom-Pom' anti-aircraft mounts were fitted on extensions of the conning-tower platform abreast the fore funnel. Above these, a pair of quadruple Mark II mountings for the 0.5-inch Vickers Mark III machine gun were added, with a maximum range of about 5,000 yards.

Repulse also received two High-Angle Control System (HACS) anti-aircraft directors, one Mark II on the foretop and a Mark I mounted on a pedestal above the rear superstructure. The HACS calculated the necessary deflection required to place a shell in the location of a target flying at a known height, bearing and speed. The two submerged torpedo tubes were removed and the vacant spaces sub-divided and turned into storerooms.

When she was recommissioned in April 1936, *Repulse* was assigned to the Mediterranean Fleet, and in late 1936 deployed to transport 500 refugees fleeing the Spanish Civil War from Valencia and Palma de Mallorca to Marseilles in France. *Repulse* was present at the Coronation Fleet Review at Spithead on 20 May 1937 for King George VI, and in July 1938 was sent to Haifa in northern Israel to maintain order during the Arab Revolt. She was again refitted between October 1938 and March 1939, this time for conveying the British King and Queen to Canada for their May 1939 Tour. At this time, the twin 4-inch anti-aircraft guns were replaced by two more Mark V guns, and two additional quadruple .50-calibre mounts were added. The King and Queen ultimately traveled aboard the liner RMS *Empress of Australia* (1919) while *Repulse* escorted them on the first half of the journey.

World War II

By the outbreak of war in September 1939, *Repulse* was part of the Battlecruiser Squadron of the British Home Fleet – and a very different ship from her original 1916 construction. In late October 1939, she was deployed to Halifax, Nova Scotia, along with the aircraft carrier HMS *Furious* (a converted World War I battlecruiser) to protect convoys and search for German surface raiders. *Repulse* and *Furious* sortied from Halifax on 23 November in search of the German battleship *Scharnhorst* after it had sunk the armed merchant cruiser HMS *Rawalpindi*, but *Repulse* was damaged by heavy seas in a storm and was forced to return to port.

Between 10 and 23 December 1939, *Repulse* escorted a large convoy bringing the 20,000 troops of the 1st Canadian Infantry Division to Britain. Thereafter she was reattached to the Home Fleet. In February 1940, she accompanied the aircraft carrier HMS *Ark Royal* on a fruitless search for six German blockade runners that had broken out of Vigo, Spain.

From April to June 1940, *Repulse* was tasked to support Allied operations during the Norwegian Campaign. On 7 April, along with the bulk of the Home Fleet, she was ordered to sea to intercept what was thought to be another attempted German breakout into the North Atlantic. *Repulse* was detached from the main British force the following day to search for German shipping reported by the destroyer HMS *Glowworm* – German destroyers were in fact transporting troops for the invasion of Norway. On 8 April, HMS *Glowworm* was sunk by the German heavy cruiser *Admiral Hipper*, and *Repulse* was subsequently ordered to rendezvous with her sister ship *Renown* south of the Lofoten Islands, off the Norwegian coast.

On 12 April, *Repulse* was ordered to return to Scapa Flow to refuel, and was put to work escorting a troop convoy upon her return. In early June, she was sent to the North Atlantic to search for German raiders. In July 1940, accompanied by *Renown* and the 1st Cruiser Squadron, *Repulse* attempted to intercept the German battleship *Gneisenau* as it sailed from Trondheim to Germany. From then until May 1941, *Repulse* was used for convoy escort duty and searches for German shipping. On 22 May 1941, she was diverted from escorting Convoy WS8B to assist in the search for the German battleship *Bismarck*, but was forced to break off the search early on 25 May as she was running low on fuel.

Captain W.G. Tennant, a tall 51-year-old grey-haired officer, took charge of her at this time. By reputation he was one of the Navy's finest captains, having served with distinction at Dunkirk where he had served ashore as senior naval officer throughout the evacuation and been one of the last to leave.

From June to August 1941, *Repulse* was again refitted at Rosyth and was equipped with eight Oerlikon 20-millimetre guns, as well as a Type 284 surface gunnery radar. As this was happening, Captain Tennant was summoned to London and told that his ship was now destined for the Indian Ocean as one of the first members of the new Eastern Fleet.

On 28 August, *Repulse* received her orders to sail as senior ship of the escort for Convoy WS11, which was to carry troops and military equipment around the Cape of Good Hope to Suez. On 31 August, *Repulse* quietly slipped out of the Forth to join her convoy, and by October 1941, she was operating in the Indian Ocean.

Repulse was assigned to Force G in November 1941, and moved across the Indian Ocean to rendezvous with *Prince of Wales* and the rest of Force G in Colombo, Ceylon. From Colombo, Force G moved on to Singapore, arriving there amid great fanfare on 2 December 1941.

Just five days later, on 7 December 1941, Japanese aircraft launched their surprise early-morning attack on the US Naval Base at Hawaii. On 8 December, Singapore was bombed by Japanese aircraft.

BOOK TWO

FORCE Z IN ACTION

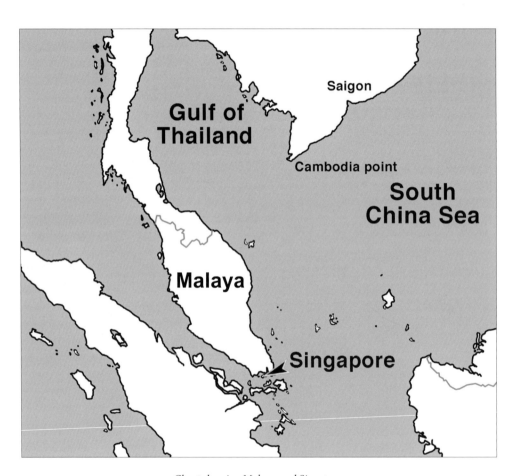

Chart showing Malaya and Singapore

CHAPTER ONE

SINGAPORE:

ISLAND CITADEL – OR CITADEL ILLUSION?

By 1818, the Dutch were the dominant traders in modern day Indonesia, Malaysia and Thailand, with many trading ports and cities throughout the scattered islands. Britain's power at this time was in the ascendancy – consolidating and opening up new links to the east. The trade route between China and British India had become vitally important with the establishment of the opium trade. The 400-mile-long Malay Peninsula lies astride the route between India and China.

Europeans had arrived in this area 400 years earlier in the 1400s. The Portuguese seized Malacca in 1511, but were supplanted by the Dutch in the 1600s. Britain, via the East India Company, gained a trading foothold in the region at Bencoolen on the south-west coast of Sumatra in 1685, and went on to firmly establish their position by building Fort Marlborough in the city in 1714. They leased Penang Island, off the north-west coast of Malaya, in 1786, and established another major trading station there.

In 1818, Sir Thomas Stamford Raffles – a name that has become synonymous with that of Singapore – was appointed Lieutenant Governor of the British colony at Bencoolen. A farsighted and strategic thinker, he believed that Britain should take steps to replace the Dutch as the dominant power in the region.

The Dutch feared the growing competition from Britain and attempted to stifle British trade in the region. They prohibited the British from trading in Dutch-controlled ports – with the sole exception of Batavia, where harsh and unfavourable prices were imposed on Britons. Raffles reasoned that the existing small British ports were unsuitable for development into major trading centres, and that the way to challenge the Dutch was to establish a major new British port in the region.

In 1818, Raffles secured funding for an expedition to establish a new British East India Company base in the region, which would protect and aid British merchant ships sailing to and from China. After many weeks of surveying and checking out possible sites, Raffles found himself at the undeveloped island of Singapore, which then had only a small Malay fishing port on it. To his keen eyes, it was immediately clear that Singapore was the obvious choice. It was situated at the southern end of the Malay Peninsula near the busy maritime thoroughfare of the Strait of Malacca. There was an excellent natural harbour, ample fresh water supplies, timber for repairing ships – and most importantly, it was not held by the Dutch. A treaty was arranged with the local ruler, the Sultan of Johor, to acquire Singapore for the East India Company.

The establishment of Singapore by the British disrupted Dutch trade interests and exacerbated the existing tensions between the two colonial powers. The Dutch claimed that the treaty signed by Sir Stamford Raffles and the Sultan of Johor was invalid, and that the Sultanate of Johor was under the Dutch sphere of influence. Questions regarding the fate of Dutch trading rights in British India also started to boil over.

In 1820, under pressure from British merchants with Far East trading interests, negotiations started between the two great colonial powers to clarify the situation in South-East Asia. This resulted in the 1824 Anglo-Dutch Treaty, which formally confirmed the status of fledgling Singapore as a British possession. Additionally, as the Dutch were not interested in developing Malacca (their main trading centre was Batavia (Jakarta) on Java) the treaty also ceded Malacca to Britain, in exchange for British Bencoolen (on Sumatra) passing to the Dutch.

The Malay world had been simply split into two parts by the two distant powers. Malaya would be ruled by Great Britain; and the Dutch would rule the East Indies (modern day Indonesia). The area north of the Malacca Strait, including Penang and Singapore, was designated as the British sphere of influence, whilst the area south of the Malacca Strait was assigned to the Dutch. Chinese junks however soon started to turn their backs on the principal Dutch port of Batavia in favour of the free trade ports operated by the British, which came to dominate trade in the region.

Singapore grew to become an important staging post for ships trading between China and India – and with the invention of the modern steamship and the opening of the Suez Canal in 1869, Singapore started to boom. From a negligible population when Raffles landed in 1818, its population was 52,891 by 1850, and the 1911 census counted 311,303 people present.

The Pacific and Singapore itself had been largely unaffected by the events of World War I. Despite being called a world war, it was a largely European war, mainly fought far away, and was of little relevance to local traders. Britain and Japan had been formal allies, having signed a mutual aid alliance in 1902, and when Britain found herself at war with Germany in 1914. Japan honoured the treaty alliance and joined Britain in attacking the German-held colony of Tsingtao on the coast of China (this was the required limit of Japan's support on the ground – as the mutual-aid clause of the alliance only required her to assist Britain in operations in India and the Far East). At sea, the Japanese Navy went further and sent several escort vessels in 1917 to assist the hard-pressed Royal Navy on convoy escort duty in the Mediterranean.

After World War I ended, Japan retained the conquered German colony of Tsingtao, and China was forced to give up other land in the area. When the ex-German colonies in the Pacific were divided amongst the victors after 1918, the Japanese were given the Marianas, the Carolines and most of the Marshall Islands. It was a fine return for the loan of a battalion of infantry and a few escort vessels to Britain.

It was, by this stage, already obvious that Japan had expansionist aims – her empire was on the move and soon this expansion started to threaten her two wartime allies, Britain and America. Both had colonies and extensive interests in the Pacific and were heavily dependent on South-East Asia, which produced three quarters of the world's raw rubber and two thirds of its tin, at the time. The question was: how to check Japanese expansionist goals without directly antagonizing the former wartime ally.

At the end of World War I, Germany was left with no battleships – they had all been scuttled and now lay at the bottom of Scapa Flow off the Orkney Islands of northern Scotland. Conversely, Britain had enough warships – but had no base in the Far East to deploy to if the Japanese Empire threatened her empire.

In post-war gloom and austerity, the British Government felt it was prohibitively expensive to maintain an Eastern Fleet in Singapore that contained capital ships. The Admiralty's solution to the Japanese problem was for a new naval base to be built in the Far East in Singapore. The capital ships of the British Home and Mediterranean Fleets would be kept in Europe and the permanent British naval presence in the Far East would be made up of smaller cruisers, destroyers and gunboats. Royal Navy capital ships would simply make flag-flying visits from time to time. It was thought that if war in the East was ever threatened, Royal Navy capital ships from the Home and Mediterranean Fleets could be rushed out to the new Singapore Naval Base to deal with any threat.

In 1923, the British Government agreed to the Admiralty proposal and announced the development of a Naval Base at Singapore. It was hoped that this would act as a deterrent to the increasingly ambitious Japanese. Construction of the base soon started but progress was very slow, as there was no immediate tangible threat (the base would only be formally opened on 15 February 1938).

In 1919, the British Government had instituted a 'ten year rule', which assumed that after the horrors of the World War I, there would not be a major war for at least the next ten years – and as a consequence, service ministries were subjected to savage spending limits.

In 1921, the Washington Naval Treaty was signed – largely provoked by Japan's expansionist goals and designed to contain them. This was a system of arms-control that pegged the Royal Navy at roughly the size of the United States Navy and placed severe restrictions on the building of new capital ships. The treaty allowed Britain and the United States a tonnage equivalent to 15 capital ships; the Japanese were allowed nine capital ships; and France and Italy five capital ships apiece. New battleship displacement was capped at 35,000 tons and the maximum gun-barrel size pegged at 16 inches.

The Japanese were pointedly displeased that they had not been granted parity with Britain and the United States, however they were partly placated by a deal whereby Britain would not develop naval bases east of Singapore and the United States would not develop bases west of Hawaii. Japan had effectively been granted control of the northwest Pacific.

After the huge costs of World War I, Britain – fearing that it could not match Japanese and American ship-building programmes – had accepted the terms of the Washington Naval Treaty. At a stroke they had abandoned their 19th-century policy that the Royal Navy must be equal in size to the world's next two largest navies.

The signing of the Washington Naval Treaty led to the scrapping of the bulk of the Royal Navy's capital ships, with few replacements being built due to economies in defence spending – and little was done to modernize the older surviving ships. Some capital ships like *Repulse* were extensively rebuilt but Britain's huge ship-building industry was crippled. Worse, the Royal Navy's lead in the new field of naval aviation was squandered.

However, the British Empire was in reality still the second strongest economic power on earth and was more than able to pay for the creation of a Far East battle fleet, given its global responsibilities. But until this time, Britain had only been concerned with the other European navies – and believed that by dominating the European naval powers, the Royal Navy could shield the Empire from interference. The signing of the Washington Naval Treaty and the acceptance of the limits it imposed effectively removed the Royal Navy's ability to protect the Empire, and signalled to the world that Britain did not take seriously a naval threat directed at the Empire rather than at Britain itself.

In a time of conflict with Japan, Britain would now be required to despatch the bulk of its capital ships to the Far East, just to meet Japan on equal terms – this would be impossible if another threat to Britain or the Empire existed elsewhere. The Empire's naval shield had been cast aside.

Despite not having enough ships, the Admiralty was directed to come up with a strategy for defending the Far East Empire – and the great trading port of Singapore – against the Japanese threat. It concluded that the main Royal Navy Fleet would only sail to Singapore if a definite threat emerged in that region. It was expected that Singapore would have to hold out for several weeks if threatened or attacked, until the Fleet arrived.

A few years later, the 1930 London Naval Treaty led to the imposition of further restrictions on the building and replacement of warships. The number of cruisers and submarines allowed to nations was restricted and an existing battleship construction holiday was extended, further eroding the Royal Navy's ability to protect the Empire.

The construction of the Singapore Naval Base proceeded slowly throughout the 1920s and 1930s with plans to build a base large enough to hold the entire Royal Navy battle fleet being shelved to save money. While Britain saw the Naval Base as vital for the *defence* of her Empire, Japanese eyes viewed the Singapore Naval Base as a British base for *aggression* against her interests.

In 1931, Japanese troops invaded Manchuria.

The League of Nations had been founded at the end of World War I, with the aim of bringing nations together and maintaining world peace – Japan was a member. At the League of Nations Assembly in Geneva on 24 February 1933, the League blamed Japan for the events in Manchuria and called for Japan to withdraw her troops and restore the country to Chinese sovereignty. The Japanese delegation, in defiance of world opinion, dramatically withdrew from the League of Nations and walked out from the hall, unwilling to accept the Assembly's report.

In 1937, Japan invaded China and the Second Sino-Japanese War started. The League of Nations and the United States (who had not joined the League) condemned the invasion. In the resulting political stand off, the US gunboat *Panay* was attacked and sunk by Japanese aircraft on 12 December 1937, while she was anchored in the Yangtze River outside Nanking (now Nanjing) in China. The Japanese claimed their pilots had not seen the American flags painted on the deck of the gunboat. Japan apologized and paid an indemnity, but great harm had been done to US-Japanese relations.

On 26 January 1938, a Japanese soldier struck John Allison – the consul at the American Embassy in Nanking – in the face. The Japanese, responding to American demands, again apologized, but this incident, coupled with the USS *Panay* incident just two months earlier and looting of American property in Nanking, increased tensions between the US and Japan even further.

Amidst all this turmoil in the Far East, and no doubt finally spurred on by it, in 1938, the British Naval Base at Singapore was finally opened, at the huge cost of some £2.5 billion at today's rates. The Naval Base was essentially a fenced off town with rows of depots, magazines and barracks. Covering 21 square miles it boasted the largest dry dock in the world, the third-largest floating dock (towed all the way from Britain), and fuel tanks to support the entire Royal Navy battle fleet for six months. There were 18 Royal Navy vessels present at the opening, in a spectacle that had the cruiser HMS *Norfolk* flying the flag of the Eastern Fleet. No battleships were present, but the new Singapore Naval Base stood ready to receive these, should the British Empire in the Far East be threatened.

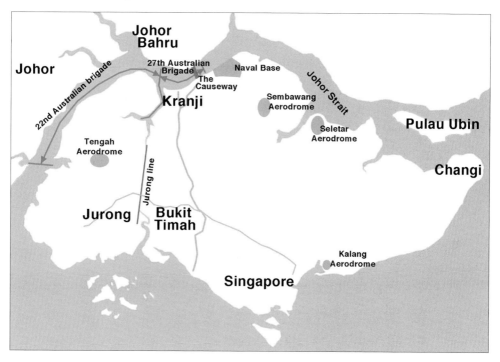

Map of Singapore Island during World War I showing Naval Base and RAF aerodromes

The world was already descending once again into chaos. In Italy, the Fascists had seized control in the 1920s, and in Germany, the Nazi Party came to power, with Hitler being appointed Chancellor in 1933. In 1935, Italy invaded Abyssinia (now Ethiopia), and in Spain, civil war broke out in 1936. In 1938, Germany re-occupied the Sudetenland, and in 1939, the Soviet-Japanese Border War started. Then, Germany invaded Poland and finally triggered World War II.

In numerical terms, Britain would soon start World War II with a seemingly impressive strength of capital ships: 12 battleships, three battlecruisers and six aircraft carriers. Five French battleships and one French carrier augmented those 21 capital ships. This combined force faced five German battleships and battlecruisers. However, in the summer of 1940, six Italian battleships were added to the Axis strength. The French Fleet, however, was soon lost to the Allies after the Fall of France in 1940. France had signed an armistice with Germany, and even though France and Britain were not at war, Britain feared that the French Fleet would fall into German hands and be turned against her. The Royal Navy therefore attacked the French Fleet at anchor in Mers-el-Kébir in French Algeria on 3 July 1940. The unsuspecting French Fleet was caught unaware and one battleship was sunk and five other ships were damaged, with the loss of 1,297 French ratings.

But of the 15 British battleships and battlecruisers, only three – *Nelson*, *Rodney* and *Hood* – were post-1918 ships; *Hood* only just so. All the German ships, however, were of modern construction – her World War I Fleet had been scuttled. Importantly, the German and Italian ships were able to feed and supply themselves from mainland Europe and could be easily kept in harbour until they were required to strike at the Royal Navy. Meanwhile, British ships were thinly stretched, guarding a huge arc from the Red Sea to Scandinavia against enemy attacks on its vital overseas trade shipping.

Construction had started in 1937 on the five new British King George V fast battleships as World War II loomed. Britain's future appeared to largely depend on these five new battleships and four new aircraft carriers, which had also started to come into service as the war started. The Germans were building only two new battleships – *Bismarck* and *Tirpitz* – and one carrier: *Graf Zeppelin*.

With war looming, defence of the Singapore Naval Base was strengthened. Two more military airfields were built in the north of Singapore Island at Tengah and Sembawang, and a further five airfields were built in northern Malaya to extend air cover out over the sea (a Japanese attack was expected to likely come from the sea and be directed only at Singapore Island itself – the jungle of mainland Malaya was thought to be difficult terrain for troops).

To deal with any seaborne attack, 12 coastal artillery batteries were installed to defend the Singapore Naval Base – some with large 15-inch naval guns and others with smaller calibre guns. These differing types of guns were classified as either 'close defence guns' or 'counter-bombardment guns'.

Close defence guns were comprised of 6-inch guns with lower 15-degree elevation mountings, 6-pounder twin guns and 12-pounder quick-firing guns. These were intended to deal with enemy warships and fast-motor torpedo-boats, which might penetrate into the close vicinity of Singapore itself to attack British shipping at anchor.

The counter-bombardment guns were intended to counter enemy battleships, heavy cruisers and light cruisers which may take station some way away from Singapore and use their big, long-range guns to bombard the port installations, dockyards and the ships alongside from a distance. The counter-bombardment guns were comprised of 6-inch guns with higher 45-degree elevation mountings, 9.2-inch guns with 35-degree elevation mountings, and the big 15-inch guns. Altogether, there were 51 coast defence guns of these various calibres installed in and around Singapore.

The big 15-inch guns were unique. With an extreme range of 24 miles, they were specifically installed to deal with distant enemy battleships of over 35,000 tons. The Johor Battery (located off Upper Changi Road) had three 15-inch guns, and the Buona Vista Battery had two 15-inch guns. Together they controlled the entire Singapore Strait.

With the Coastal Batteries, the Royal Air Force airfields and the Naval Base facility to hold capital ships, Winston Churchill famously called Singapore the 'Gibraltar of the East'. Others called it 'Fortress Singapore'. But in truth, little had been spent on shore-defences and the army and RAF strength was slender. In an attack, Singapore would have to hold off the Japanese until the big ships of the Royal Navy arrived.

Officially, the period Singapore was expected to withstand a siege before relief came in the form of the Royal Navy's main battle fleet, was 42 days. By 1939, this period had been raised to 70 days – and then to 90 days, and ultimately 180 days. It was clear that the army and the RAF were going to have to shoulder a greater burden of Malaya's defence in the navy's absence.

'Fortress Singapore' it may have been, but it was a fortress without a fleet to protect it. The defence of the British homeland would come first in any conflict, and the Mediterranean with its vital oil and trade communications took second place. The Royal Navy capital ships would be retained in the Home Fleet and Mediterranean Fleet. The threat by Japan to the Far East came only third, and nothing larger than a cruiser was allocated to the Far East.

British authorities knew that defence of Singapore was a problem. A 1939 British Chief of Staff (COS) Sub Committee Report (CAB 53/50) stated that to effectively hold Singapore, Britain would need to deploy at least eight capital ships for use against an estimated nine Japanese battleships and battlecruisers which could be ranged against the Royal Navy. Such a large British force would never be available if Britain was at war with Germany – and in this latter scenario, the report concluded that it would only be possible to send two capital ships to Singapore. If hostilities then flared up around Singapore, those two capital ships would be vulnerable and would require to retreat to a safer base.

The COS Report also concluded that if the Japanese fleet moved southwards in force, Royal Navy forces at Singapore would require to retire westward – leaving Singapore open to capture. A Royal Navy Fleet would then require to be formed up and sent to relieve Singapore. Such a relief fleet could only be created by taking ships from both Mediterranean and Home Waters, and this would leave only three capital ships at home – quite an unacceptable situation. The report concluded that if the Japanese successfully took Singapore, it would be futile to attempt to recapture it.

It is often stated that the big guns protecting Singapore pointed only to the sea – but this is not correct. The big guns of Singapore were not pointed the wrong way. True, they had been installed primarily for the seaward defence of Singapore and to protect the Naval Base – indeed, the fact that there was no direct naval attack would appear to demonstrate that their deterrent effect was successful. Perhaps with Singapore's guns in mind, Japanese strategic plans for the invasion of Singapore provided for a land-based assault from the north. No Japanese warships were deployed during the Battle of Singapore.

Except for two of the big 15-inch guns, all the other guns had all-round traverse and could – and did – fire landwards at Japanese targets in Johor on the mainland and on Singapore Island. Observation of the fall of fire was difficult, however, the field-of-view inland being limited. However, no land-service high-explosive shells were provided for the 15-inch guns – the only supply of ammunition provided being armour-piercing shells for use against ships.

In addition to the reinforcement of the island against attack from the sea, British military planners had in fact also anticipated a Japanese attack on Singapore from the rear down the Malay Peninsula. Operation Matador had been conceived and created to directly counter this threat. In Operation Matador, British land forces would enter southern Thailand to thwart Japanese landings on the eastern coastline. The concept of this forward defence had been put forward as early as 1918, well before the idea of the Singapore naval base had been conceived. The essence of the strategy was that to ensure the landward security of Singapore, the whole of the Malayan mainland must be held. During 1940, troops began to clear swamps and undergrowth and install barbed wire posts on the beaches along the south coast of Singapore.

Operation Matador gained official British approval in 1941, but the resources for its implementation – critical aircraft and other reinforcements – were never provided. Defence of Singapore and Malaya was placed below the Middle East and Russia in terms of priorities. The war in the Middle East, which was the world's oil pipeline and gateway to India, was not going well for the Allies, and Russian vulnerability added to the complexities of the situation. The battle for Malaya and Singapore had been lost in the corridors of power at Whitehall, before the first shot was fired. Bureaucrats over-emphasised the impregnability of the British fortress of Singapore and underestimated the Japanese threat.

In 1941, 440 aircraft were delivered to Russia despite a belief amongst chiefs of staff that, on purely military grounds, they would 'pay a better dividend' if sent to the Far East or the Middle East. An entire division which was bound for Singapore – the 7th Australian Division – was diverted to the Middle East, as well as one brigade of the 9th Indian Division to Iraq, to quell a revolt there.

In September 1939, the principal infantry units of the Malayan garrison were the 2nd Loyals, 1st Manchesters, 2nd Gordon Highlanders, 2/17th Dogras, and 1st Malays. During 1939–41 however, regular British Army units in Malaya were forced to send large drafts of soldiers back to Britain to serve in other units of their regiment or corps, and to accept less suitable National Service conscripts as replacements.

Most of the troops who arrived in Malaya after 1939 were from India. In February 1941, the first Australian troops arrived on the *Queen Mary*. As a dominion of the British Empire, Australia had immediately followed Britain into the war with Germany in September 1939.

On 22 June 1941, Germany invaded the Soviet Union, and with Russia (a country with which Japan had a long history of conflict) now concentrated on fighting off the Nazis, Japan was free to consider a more aggressive policy in South-East Asia.

On 2 July 1941, the Imperial Conference in Tokyo agreed to 'construct the Greater East Asia Co-prosperity Sphere regardless of the changes in the world situation'. Japan resolved to continue the war in China, to await developments with Russia, and to prepare for an expansion into South-East Asia. The next step would be the establishment of military bases in southern Indochina (modern-day Cambodia, Laos and Vietnam). France had controlled Vietnam since the latter part of the 19th century but with war in Europe and the fall of France in 1940, the French hold on Indochina was weak.

On 14 July 1941, the French authorities in Indochina were given a set of Japanese demands, which – with little room to manoeuvre – were accepted on 23 July and heralded the arrival in the region of the first of tens of thousands of Japanese troops. Japanese warships were stationed at coastal ports and air force units were stationed around Saigon. Once the Japanese had established themselves in southern Indochina, they were closer than ever to Singapore, the Philippines and Dutch East Indies.

The USA reacted to the latest demonstration of Japanese aggression on the Asian mainland on 25 July, by banning the export to Japan of the oil and other materials that had been fuelling the Japanese war machine for years. During the 1930s, Japan had imported half its oil from America, and by 1940–41 it was importing 80% of its oil from America and 10% from the East Indies. Japan had been stockpiling oil – but only had sufficient for 18 months usage at normal rates. America also introduced an asset freeze, which prevented the Japanese from obtaining the dollars they needed to buy American goods. British and Dutch governments soon followed their lead.

In June 1941, a German invasion of Britain was still considered a strong possibility by military planners, and so the home defence of Britain still took precedence. British officials thought that the Russians would not last long against the might of the Nazi war machine that had so easily conquered France. There appeared to be sufficient time for the German army to beat the Russians and return to Europe to invade Britain before winter. But as 1941 wore on, it started to become clear that the Soviets were managing to hold on and that no invasion of Britain would be possible that year. An invasion attempt was thought likely in the following Spring of 1942 – so the War Office still could not run any risk to the defence of Britain itself.

Lt. General Arthur Percival, General Officer Commanding (Malaya). (IWM)

Early in August 1941, the newly appointed Lt. General Arthur Percival was just beginning his posting as General Officer Commanding (Malaya) in command of the British & Commonwealth forces at Singapore. He reported to the War Office that his minimum requirements in Malaya were five divisions of troops and an armoured brigade. In late August and September, the 27th Australian and 28th Indian Brigades reached Singapore – they would be the last significant formations Percival would receive that year. The 5th, 88th and 137th Field Regiments, along with the 80th Anti-Tank Regiment, were due to arrive late in November and early December. By November 1941, however, Percival only had four under-strength divisions under his command; less than the five he required as a minimum.

The RAF was unable to implement its pledge to build up RAF strength in Malaya. A handful of new fighter squadrons were indeed formed in Malaya, but were equipped with American-built 323mph Brewster F2A Buffalo fighter aircraft. These had been rejected for service in Britain because of fuel starvation issues above 15,000 feet, but, desperate for fighters for the Pacific and Asia, a number had been ordered from America by Britain. The Buffalo was to be shown to be no match for the Japanese Zero fighter in combat, and was criticised for lack of armament and pilot armour, poor high-altitude performance, engine over-heating, and poor maintenance and cockpit controls (although it did win praise for its handling, roomy cockpit and visibility).

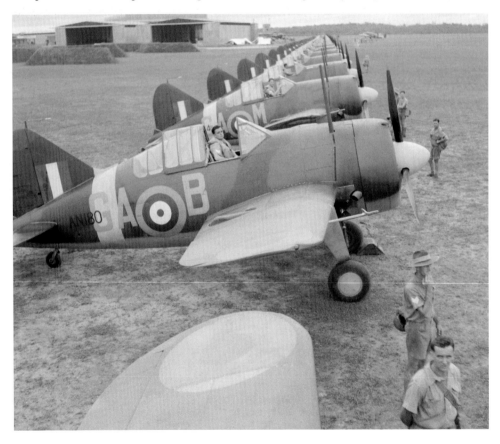

Brewster Buffalo Mark I fighter aircraft of No 21 Squadron RAAF, lined up at Sembawang, Singapore.
(IWM)

By the end of 1941, the RAF had only 158 aircraft in Malaya, with another 88 in reserve.

From late August 1941, Churchill had been urging the Admiralty to send a small force of capital ships to Singapore, and managed to push the plan through despite the Admiralty's preferred plan of building up an Eastern Fleet in the Indian Ocean during 1942. Churchill had always conceded that the creation of a small Far Eastern Squadron was as much a political, as a naval, gesture.

Percival disposed his under-strength forces for the defence of Malaya. The 9th Indian Division's two brigades were posted on the east coast at Kota Bharu and Kuantan, to defend the air bases recently constructed there. The 11th Indian Division's two brigades were posted in north-west Malaya at Jitra, from where they could advance into Thailand towards Singora as part of Operation Matador; or take up a defensive position to shield Alor Setar air base. The 12th Indian Brigade was held in reserve, south of Kuala Lumpur.

The two Australian Brigades were stationed in Johor, just across the causeway connecting the north of Singapore Island to mainland Malaya. At Singapore itself, the garrison fielded another two brigades of regular troops. By 1 December 1941, the Malaya army force reached 91,000, and would be boosted on the arrival of a convoy on 7 December.

Meanwhile, preparations for the pre-emptive invasion of southern Thailand, under Operation Matador, to thwart any Japanese invasion proceeded apace, and 30 or more officers were sent into Thailand with civilian identities to reconnoitre.

Fortress Singapore exuded a feeling of security in these pre-war days. The island had been heavily fortified: there were troops everywhere and uniforms of all kinds seen on the streets. Aircraft droned overhead incessantly, and at night the sky was criss-crossed by searchlight beams. By day and night, firing practice from the 15-inch guns could be heard. Singapore felt like a citadel island – but was that merely an illusion?

CHAPTER TWO

THE JAPANESE THREAT

As the closing years of the 19th century gave way to the 20th century, it was a time of great industrial change. Japan – a small island country with limited natural resources of its own – was determined to become a modern, industrial nation and avoid the fate of China. By the middle of the 19th century, European powers had forced the weakened Chinese Empire to open its doors to trade, and the Chinese coast had become dominated by European trading posts such as Hong Kong and Shanghai.

The opening up of Japan to western trade in the 19th century had, to an extent, put Japan on a similar path. Japan's leaders, however, did not want Japan to become an economic plaything of the great Western powers – like China had become – and set out to modernize: the pace of that change was extraordinary. Japan admired and envied the naval power and dominance of Great Britain, and Japanese naval reform was largely based on the Royal Navy template. Japan grew in power and influence but she was an industrial nation heavily dependent on imported raw materials.

The proximity of China and Russia on the Asian mainland to the west had always been a threat to Japan's security. Under the Treaty of Beijing in 1860, Russia acquired from China a large Pacific coast Maritime Province adjacent to northern Japan, along with the island of Sakhalin. China had just lost the Opium War with Britain and was unable to defend the region. Shortly afterwards, the first buildings of the present day port city of Vladivostok were erected.

In the 1890s, Russia began building the Trans-Siberian Railway to Vladivostok. There was no economic justification for building the railway – it was an overtly strategic endeavor, which would allow Russia to transport and maintain a large army near its Pacific coast. Fear of Russia became a dominant feature of Japanese foreign policy from then on.

In 1896, Russia signed an alliance with China against Japan, and took a lease of Port Arthur – a strategically vital Chinese Manchurian port to the south of Korea. Three years later in 1899, Russia began building a branch of the Trans-Siberian railway to Port Arthur, and continued to build up its military strength in Manchuria. Their Pacific Fleet was then moved to Port Arthur. Russia had obvious territorial ambitions, which Japan viewed with grave fear.

Britain and Japan signed a defensive alliance in 1902, and on 8 February 1904 Japan initiated the Russo-Japanese War, with a surprise torpedo boat destroyer attack on the Russian Fleet at Port Arthur which badly damaged several of the heavier Russian naval vessels. Japanese forces from Korea also landed on the Manchurian coast and swiftly cut off Port Arthur. In a series of fierce land-battles, Russian forces were pushed northwards across Manchuria. Port Arthur fell after a bloody siege in January 1905. Russia was forced to send its Baltic Fleet half way round the world to relieve its beleaguered Far East Fleet. The Baltic Fleet left European waters in late 1904 and passed Singapore on 8 April 1905.

The final land-battle of this war was fought at Mukden in February and March 1905, between Russian forces totaling 330,000 men and Japanese totaling 270,000. After long and heavy fighting, the Russian army broke off and withdrew northwards, allowing Mukden to fall into Japanese hands.

The Japanese had found themselves unable to secure the complete command of the sea that their land campaign depended on, and the Russian Naval Squadrons at Port Arthur and Vladivostok remained active. On 27–29 May 1905, the Japanese Fleet under Admiral Togo won a historic victory at the Battle of Tsushima, when it destroyed the recently arrived Russian Baltic Fleet. The battle was won by a Japanese navy created with British technical assistance, and warships built mainly at British shipyards.

The Tsarist Government signed a peace treaty with Japan in September 1905, in which Japan secured the rights in Manchuria that had been Russia's – including Port Arthur and the southern section of the Manchurian railway. They now had vested interests and possessions in Manchuria to protect.

During World War I, the 1902 Anglo-Japanese alliance encouraged Japan to enter the war against Germany. Still intent on expansion and gaining territories and raw materials, they quickly seized German possessions in China and the Pacific.

The Great Depression from 1929 onwards and the subsequent collapse in world trade hit Japan's export-orientated economy hard. The economic crisis led to the Japanese military becoming increasingly convinced that Japan needed guaranteed access to new markets and raw materials on the Asian mainland. Japan's population had more than doubled and demand was high.

On 14 November 1930, an assassination attempt was made on Prime Minister Osachi Hamaguchi, when a member of an ultra-nationalist group shot him in Tokyo Station. During the negotiations towards the London Naval Conference Treaty earlier in 1930, he had tried – but failed – to secure a better ratio of battleships for Japan in comparison to Great Britain and the USA. His failure and settlement of the treaty led to a feeling that he had sold out Japanese national security, and prompted a surge of Japanese nationalism. Hamaguchi was hospitalised for several months. He returned to office on 10 March 1931, but resigned a month later.

With Hamaguchi's firm rule no longer at the helm, a growing militarism took a firm hold in Japanese politics. Just six months after Hamaguchi's resignation, the local warlord in Manchuria formally recognised the Chinese Nationalist Government in Nanking, and began to obstruct the Japanese presence in southern Manchuria – which they had possessed since the 1905 Russo-Japan War. (By the late 1920s, after years of development, three quarters of the region's economy was in Japanese hands, and it was a major source of coal and iron ore for Japan, as well as being an important export market.)

With Japan's vital economic position in Manchuria at risk, on 18 September 1931, officers of the Kwantung Army (the Japanese forces in Manchuria) took matters into their own hands.

Without advising their commander-in-chief or the Tokyo civilian government, the officers staged a bombing incident on a railway they were guarding near the town of Mukden.

The Kwantung Army claimed that local Chinese forces were responsible and launched a campaign against them. They shelled the local Chinese garrison and destroyed the small Chinese air force. Five-hundred battle-hardened Japanese troops assaulted the garrison of some 7,000 Chinese troops (mostly irregulars or conscripts). The fighting was over by the evening and the Japanese occupied Mukden at the cost of 500 Chinese dead and two Japanese dead. The Japanese then went on to occupy the major Manchurian cities of Changchun and Antung and surrounding areas, and established a puppet state. The Tokyo civilian government was forced to rubber stamp the military's actions after the event.

The Chinese appealed to the League of Nations – of which they were members – for a peaceful solution. The League of Nations started to investigate the war in Manchuria and whilst these investigations were ongoing, Prime Minister Inukai Tsuyoshi came to power on 13 December 1931. He tried to place fiscal restraints on the military, but failed. He was also unable to control the military's designs on China. Early in 1932, a large Japanese expeditionary force was sent to Shanghai to counter anti-Japanese riots. The fighting lasted for weeks.

A *coup d'état* in Japan was staged on 15 May 1932, launched by reactionary elements of the Japanese Imperial Navy. Eleven young naval officers assassinated Prime Minister Tsuyoshi and brought the civilian government to its knees: the military was now in control of Japan. Now unchecked, massive increases in Japanese military spending started and these would continue throughout the 1930s.

At the League of Nations Assembly in Geneva on 24 February 1933, the League called for Japan to withdraw her troops and restore Manchuria to Chinese sovereignty. The Japanese delegation, in defiance of world opinion, dramatically withdrew from the League of Nations and walked out from the hall, unwilling to accept the Assembly's report. Their isolation from the community of nations had started.

In Europe, Hitler came to power in 1933. Nazi Germany left the League of Nations that year, and repudiated the military clauses of the 1919 Treaty of Versailles. The system of naval disarmament instituted after World War I in terms of the Versailles Treaty was in tatters.

In June 1935, in an effort to control the situation, an Anglo-German naval treaty was negotiated, in which Britain agreed that Germany could build a fleet of up to 35% of the Royal Navy's surface tonnage. Although not clear at the time, with the rebirth of the German Fleet, it had just become unlikely that the Royal Navy could ever send a large naval force to the Far East – and Malaya in particular. A number of old general naval treaties were due to expire in 1936 and negotiations took place in 1935–36 for a new round of treaties. Japan, however, withdrew from the negotiations.

In the mid 1930s, more than half of Britain's battleships and aircraft carriers were un-modernised or obsolete. As the political situation became increasingly unstable an expansion programme for the Royal Navy and RAF was finally initiated. But the new Royal Navy vessels, which would be launched in the late 1930s and 40s under this expansion programme, would only replace old ships – doing nothing to increase Britain's overall naval vessel numbers, and thus doing nothing to allow it to meet the combined maritime threats of Germany in Europe and Japan in the Far East.

The Japanese government was determined to follow a policy of expansion – called the

'Greater East Asia Co-Prosperity Sphere'. Central to that policy was the extension of Japanese power and the acquisition of an empire similar to those of the European powers. Japan's lack of her own oil resources was a critical vulnerability and caused Japan to eye the oil-rich Dutch East Indies (now Indonesia) with particular interest.

The Second Sino-Japanese War started on 7 July 1937, when Japan initially assaulted a crucial access point to Beijing. The Japanese went on to capture the city of Beijing itself, as well as Tianjin – showing great brutality to Chinese soldiers and civilians alike. After the Battle of Shanghai, defeated Chinese troops were forced to retreat along the Yangtze basin towards the Nationalist capital of Nanking, 200 miles upriver from Shanghai, all the time being pressed by Japanese mechanised columns and aircraft. Japanese forces soon arrived outside Nanking.

On 8 December 1937, the Japanese ordered the Chinese army defending the city to surrender, by noon on 10 December. Come 10 December, when the Chinese defending forces did not surrender, the Japanese attack began. After two days of resistance, the Japanese successfully took the city on 13 December.

As soon as they entered the city, Japanese troops embarked on an officially condoned terror campaign against the civilian population in and around the city – which became known as the 'Rape of Nanking'. What began as an operation to round up and kill Chinese soldiers, turned into a drunken orgy of murder and rape. Bodies were dumped in the Yangtze River, washing up downstream on the banks. Japanese soldiers used Chinese prisoners for public displays of bayonet practice before crowds of horrified onlookers. There were beheading competitions and the gang-rape of thousands of women, who were shot afterwards. Chinese propagandists claimed at the time, that some 250,000 people were killed at Nanking – Western observers put the numbers in the tens of thousands. The indiscriminate total war of the Second Sino-Japanese War would continue through to the end of World War II.

The Soviet Union began to aid China – hoping that by keeping China in the war with Japan, it would stop Japan from invading Siberia. This policy led to Japan becoming engaged in military confrontation with Russian troops along the Manchurian-Siberian frontier – fighting which would last until an armistice was declared in September 1939.

Japan, with scarce raw materials and resources of her own, had largely depended on American exports of oil and iron. Ironically, it was American trade and exports throughout the 1930s which had largely underpinned Japan's war industries and allowed Japan to wage her wars of aggression. But American tolerance of Japanese aggression was wearing thin. American public opinion turned sharply against Japan after her aircraft sunk the US Navy gunboat *Panay* on 12 December 1937 at anchor in the Chinese Yangtze River. Two months later the US consul in Nanking was attacked and American property looted.

Contrary to what she sought to achieve by securing her own resources in Manchuria and China, Japan's China Policy, far from making her self-sufficient by securing raw materials, was in fact making her more dependent than ever on imports from the west. The weak American and British response to Japan's war in China did much to make Japanese leaders believe that Western democracies were weak and lacked resolve. The Japanese, however, were becoming battle-hardened and ruthless, as the war in China dragged on.

On 26 July 1939, after continued attacks by the Japanese military on American citizens and the encroachment on American interests in China, the United States withdrew from the US-Japan Treaty of Commerce and Navigation, which regulated trade between the two countries. Then, in the spring of 1940, conscious of the developing Japanese threat and in a move that would have great significance (unforeseen at the time), the United States Pacific Fleet moved its main base from California further west into the Pacific – to Hawaii.

In June 1940, just a month after the Fall of France, Japan demanded that her troops in China be allowed to move into the northern part of French Indochina and establish bases there, asserting her interest by direct dominance of the region. The French governor-general had to agree.

On 2 July 1940, US President Roosevelt signed the Export Control Act, which authorised licencing or prohibitioning of the export of essential defence materials. On 31 July, exports of aviation motor fuels, iron and steel were restricted. On 16 October, in a move clearly aimed at Japan, an embargo was placed on all exports of scrap iron and steel to destinations other than Britain and the nations of the Western hemisphere.

Japan was boxed into a corner – what would it do?

CHAPTER THREE

SS *AUTOMEDON* AND ITS AFTERMATH

In August 1940, in response to the ever-growing Japanese threat, a further British Chief of Staff Far Eastern Appreciation COS (40) 302 was compiled. This 28-page document was equally as pessimistic as the earlier 1939 Chief of Staff Report – which had concluded that Britain would need to deploy at least eight capital ships for use against the estimated nine Japanese battleships and battlecruisers that were available to mount an attack on Singapore.

In 1939, it had been generally accepted that such a large British naval force would never be available if Britain was at war with Germany – as it was now. In this scenario, the European war against Germany would take precedence, and it would only be possible to send two capital ships to Singapore.

The 7,528-ton SS Automedon *– selected to carry the Chiefs of Staff Report to Singapore*

Air Chief Marshal, Sir Cyril Newall of the Chiefs of Staff ordered that a copy of this August 1940 COS Appreciation be sent to Singapore to the Commander in Chief Far East, Air Chief Marshal Sir Robert Brooke Popham. The 7,528-ton Blue Funnel Line merchant ship SS *Automedon* was selected to carry the COS Report. She was scheduled to depart from Liverpool on 24 September 1940 on a routine voyage to Penang, Singapore, Hong Kong and Shanghai, carrying a general cargo of crated aircraft, machinery, vehicles, foodstuffs and 120 mail bags, which included the latest merchant navy code-deciphering tables.

A slender green canvas bag containing a full copy of the 28-page August 1940 COS Far Eastern Appreciation was duly placed aboard and locked in a drawer in the chart room of the bridge.

After departing Liverpool on 24 September 1940, the voyage went uneventfully until the evening of 10 November 1940, when in the Strait of Java, her wireless operator picked up a distress call from the Norwegian tanker *Ole Jacob*, broadcasting that an unknown ship had turned and was pursuing it. A further signal followed shortly afterwards: 'Stopped by unknown ship'. The *Ole Jacob* had been pounced on by a German commerce raider.

The remainder of the night passed without further incident and as dawn broke on 11 November, *Automedon* was some 250 miles off the north-west tip of Sumatra. Lookouts spotted the silhouette of a merchant ship off the port bow, which the captain took to be Dutch. The unidentified ship continued steaming towards *Automedon*, and an hour later the range was down to 4,600 yds.

Suddenly, at 8.20 a.m., the early morning calm was shattered as a warning shot screamed across *Automedon*'s bow. This was clearly not a Dutch merchant ship – it was the most successful German raider of World War II: the 7,862 grt auxiliary cruiser *Atlantis* and it had just raised a German battle flag.

The *Atlantis* had originally been laid down as the 155-metre long transport ship *Goldenfels* in 1937, but she had been commissioned as an auxiliary cruiser in 1939 and fitted out with 5.9-inch guns, torpedo tubes, *Heinkel* float planes and 92 mines. With a speed of 16 knots, she could easily outpace and overhaul the average steamship of the day, and after being fitted with a second dummy funnel, she looked like an inoffensive large steamship until she got so close that escape was impossible.

The seemingly innocuous German auxiliary cruiser and commerce raider Atlantis

The bridge and concealed gun platforms of the German auxiliary cruiser Atlantis

As soon as the warning shot had been fired and the unknown ship had been identified as a German raider, the wireless operator aboard *Automedon* started broadcasting that she was 'under attack by armed raider'. No doubt picking up the broadcast, and by now just 2,000 yards away, *Atlantis* responded by turning her big guns on *Automedon*, quickly destroying her emergency dynamo house and causing substantial damage throughout the ship. Seconds later, the Germans jammed *Automedon*'s distress call.

After just three minutes of unequal action, *Automedon* was a listing hulk with six of her crew dead and 12 injured. The bridge and accommodation quarters had been badly damaged and all lifeboats destroyed. *Atlantis* ceased fire.

The attack in the Strait of Java had taken place in a relatively busy shipping lane, and so the Germans wasted little time in boarding their prize. The boarding party went immediately to the strong room, where after blowing the door open with plastic explosive, 15 bags of secret mail including decoding tables, fleet orders, gunnery instructions and Naval Intelligence reports were found.

In the debris of the battered bridge, in the chart room, a weighted green canvas bag with brass eyelets (to let water in and hasten its sinking if it had to be ditched) was found in a drawer. It was marked 'Highly Confidential – to be destroyed'. The officers responsible for throwing it overboard had all been killed in the attack.

Inside, was a long narrow envelope addressed to: 'The C in C Far East. To be Opened Personally'. The envelope held what bore to be a secret report, 'TO BE KEPT UNDER LOCK AND KEY'. The secret report was in fact the latest British Far Eastern Appreciation (COS (40) 302) of the military strength of the Empire in the Far East. There were details of Royal Air Force units, naval strength, an assessment of the role of Australia and New Zealand, and official views on the possibility of Japan entering the war, along with details of the fortifications of Singapore.

Captain Rogge, in command of *Atlantis*, was fluent in English and soon realised the importance of this intelligence windfall – which also contained new cipher tables for the British Fleet, information on minefields and swept channels, maps and charts, and British Secret Service reports. He transferred the documents onto the recently acquired prize ship *Ole Jacob*, now under the charge of Lieutenant Commander Paul Kamenz and six of the *Atlantis's* crew (who now also controlled the *Ole Jacob's* Norwegian crew, as well as the crew of another Norwegian merchantman sunk by *Atlantis* a few days earlier).

The *Ole Jacob* arrived in Kobe, Japan, on December 4 1940. Within an hour of docking, German officials called to collect the documents and deliver them to the German naval attaché in Tokyo, who, on seeing them, sent a highly detailed four-part cipher telegram to Naval H/Q Berlin.

On December 6 1940, after copies had been made, a courier journeyed by train through then neutral Russia and on to Germany. On arrival in Berlin, a copy was sent to Captain Yokai, the Japanese naval attaché in Berlin, and on December 12 1940, he sent a summary of the contents to the chief of Third Section, Naval Staff, Tokyo. He commented that from the documents seized, it appeared that the present war situation would not allow Britain to send her fleet to the Far East if Singapore was threatened – and that Britain would be required to defend it by sending army and Air Force reinforcements. The same evening in Tokyo, the original report was handed to Japan's Vice Admiral Kondo, who commented: 'Such a significant weakening of the British Empire could not have been identified from outward appearances'.

Initially, the Japanese were sceptical of the report's contents, believing it to be a German ploy designed to coax them into military action against Britain – but soon the report was regarded as authentic and indicative of British policy in the Far East. Japan now believed that Britain would not go to war with her, as long as Japan confined itself to advancing into French Indochina; and that war would become inevitable if Japan should advance into the Dutch East Indies. Japan now adopted an expansionist attitude towards southern Indochina.

CHAPTER FOUR

FORCE Z IS CONCEIVED

In April 1941, under German and Japanese pressure, the Vichy government in France allowed Japan the use of air and naval bases in southern Indochina. Without firing a shot, the Japanese had secured bases only 450 miles from Malaya and 700 miles (less than the length of Britain) from Singapore. These British possessions were now well within range of Japanese bombers. Japan soon had over 400 land-based aircraft based in Indochina and 280 carrier-based aircraft available in addition. British air strength in Singapore and Malaya totalled 88 aircraft – of which only 48 were modern machines.

In July 1941, Japan demanded further military and economic concessions from France in Indochina, and this brought Japanese army units much closer to the Americans in the Philippines and the British in Malaya. On 26 July 1941, faced with this growing Japanese aggression and expansionism, Japanese assets in the USA were frozen, bringing commercial relations between the USA and Japan to an end. Exports of such grades of oil as were still in commercial flow to Japan were also embargoed shortly afterwards. Britain and Holland followed suit with trade embargoes on Japan from their colonies in south-east Asia. Japan was now isolated from the West and desperately in need of raw materials to keep her expansionist war machine in China operating.

Japan was now in an untenable position, and Britain and America knew that Japan might well try to escape the stranglehold of the embargoes by going to war. For their part, the Japanese felt that to save their empire they must take measures to secure the raw materials she needed.

Just months after the intelligence disaster of SS *Automedon*, in mid-August 1941 – and following the successful sinking of the *Bismarck* in May 1941, to counter the perceived threat of war with Japan, the British Admiralty proposed to form a Far East Fleet to be made up of seven capital ships: *Nelson*; *Rodney*; the obsolescent R-class battleships *Ramillies*; *Resolution*; *Revenge*; *Royal Sovereign*; and the recently modernised battlecruiser HMS *Renown*. None of the new fast King George V-class battleships were included.

Churchill responded to the Admiralty's proposal for a Far East Fleet by issuing a long memorandum to the Admiralty, in which he indicated that he would not approve the establishment of such a large fleet. His preferred course of action for combating the numerically superior Japanese forces was to create a small British naval force in the Indian Ocean, made up of some of the latest and most powerful ships in the Royal Navy. In one of his 'Action This Day' personal minutes sent to the First Sea Lord, he commented:

> It should become possible in the near future to place a deterrent squadron in the Indian Ocean. Such a force should consist of the smallest number of the best ships. The most economical disposition would be to send *Duke of York*, as soon as she is clear of constructional defects, via Trinidad and Simonstown to the East. She could be joined by *Repulse* or *Renown* and one aircraft carrier of high speed. This powerful force might show itself in the triangle Aden-Singapore-Simonstown. It would exert a paralysing effect upon Japanese Naval action…

Although the *Bismarck* had been sunk, Churchill weighed in the balance that the German battleships *Scharnhorst*, *Gneisenau* and the heavy cruiser *Prinz Eugen* were at Brest, on the west coast of France, and the 42,200-ton battleship *Tirpitz* and the heavy cruiser *Admiral Scheer* were believed ready for sea at their Norwegian bases. The Royal Navy had to meet the pressing demands of the Home Fleet, Gibraltar and the Mediterranean Fleet, and was hard pressed to spare more than two capital ships. He thought the formation of a large Far East Fleet only possible if America increased their present Atlantic force of three battleships to safeguard essential Allied supply convoys from America against the threat of the German raiders. If and when Britain's Far Eastern Fleet came to being, Churchill wanted it to operate primarily in the Indian Ocean.

Churchill did not fear a direct Japanese attack on Singapore or Malaya, and he did not know that the Japanese were already planning such an attack. He saw the greatest danger being from Japanese warships attacking British trade shipping in the Pacific or Indian Oceans. He wanted a fast 'hunting-down' squadron along the lines of the force that had so recently destroyed the *Bismarck*. The Admiralty, on the other hand, wanted a larger defensive force of ships to protect Malaya and Singapore.

Churchill hoped that the existence of a fast and powerful raiding squadron would have a paralysing effect on the Japanese Imperial Fleet, similar to the paralysing effect the mere presence of the *Tirpitz* in Norway had on the Royal Navy in the Atlantic. He conceded that the force could be beefed up as and when necessary, by the dispatch of four R-class battleships to the Far East, primarily to act as convoy escorts.

At first, Churchill's proposal to include *Duke of York* – one of the new King George V-class battleships – as part of his squadron, did not find favour with the Admiralty. They wanted to keep their three brand new King George V-class battleships – *Duke of York*, *Prince of Wales* and *King George V* – in the Atlantic to counter the threat posed to shipping by the modern fast German raiders *Tirpitz*, *Scharnhorst*, and *Gneisenau*.

Admiral of the Fleet Sir John Tovey resisted the dispatch of any of the new King George V-class battleships to tropical regions on the basis that the ships' ventilation systems were not designed to work in such hot climates. He also felt that the evaporators were not designed for extended periods at sea and that the variable speed gears for the 14-inch gun turrets would not work effectively under tropical conditions.

By October 1941 no one could ignore the developing events in the Far East, and following an (at times) sharp exchange between Churchill and the Admiralty, on 20 October 1941, the Admiralty gave way to Churchill's plan for a small powerful force, in preference to their wish for a larger fleet. The *Prince of Wales*, which had cut its teeth in the *Bismarck* action, was chosen in reference to the *Duke of York*, which it was felt was too new and unready. The battlecruiser *Repulse*, already operating in the Indian Ocean, was selected along with the new aircraft carrier *Indomitable*.

Force Z had become a reality and the lives of hundreds of the crew of these ships – and indeed the fate of Singapore itself – had just been determined.

CHAPTER FIVE

JAPAN GAMBLES TO SECURE AN EMPIRE AND ITS RESOURCES

Germany's speedy and brutal conquest of most of continental Europe had clearly demonstrated that she was the strongest power in Europe. Throughout the 1930s, Japan had been building closer relations with Germany, and so, with Germany at the peak of its power, the moment seemed ideal for Japan to form an alliance with her.

Faced with crippling trade embargoes by America, Britain and Holland in July 1941, Japan entered the Axis Pact with Germany and Italy on 27 September 1941. In the pact, Germany, Italy and Japan agreed to aid each other if one of their number was attacked by a power not involved in a current conflict.

Membership of the Axis Pact for Japan ensured that Germany recognised that East Asia was a Japanese sphere of influence. Germany and Italy intended to establish a New Order in Europe – Japan would do likewise in Greater East Asia.

Germany, for her part, hoped that Japan would restrain America whilst she dealt a final knock out blow to Britain. The Axis Pact enabled Japan's leaders to consider the possibility of simultaneous war with America and Britain more seriously. Japan's entry into the Axis Pact led America and Britain to increasingly view Germany and Japan as a joint threat.

With an eye on a future conflict in the region, Japanese officers disguised as commercial travellers had been sent into South-East Asia throughout 1941 to gather intelligence. British officers had likewise been sent. In Thailand, British and Japanese agents were known to have stayed in the same hotels. Every town in Malaya had Japanese businessmen, shop keepers, dentists and the like, some of whom were providing material to the Japanese; and in Singapore, Japanese residents provided aerial photographs of Singapore to Japan. New Japanese air bases were built in southern Indochina to support the oncoming offensive.

Japanese assessments of intelligence reports and information gathered concluded that Singapore's southern sea-facing defences were sound and should not be attacked. The big land-based British guns had served their deterrent role. But the Japanese were less impressed by the military preparations in Johor and the north coast of Singapore.

At the Japanese Imperial Conference on 6 September 1941, in the presence of the Emperor, it was decided to complete war preparations by the end of October. Meantime, Japan would continue negotiations with the USA in an attempt to end the trade embargo. It was felt that if Japan did nothing, the slow strangulation of the trade embargoes would cause the country to collapse in a few years, for lack of raw materials.

If the embargoes could not be lifted, Japan would go to war – and she believed she had a 70–80% chance of initial victory. A successful war against the Western powers would allow Japan to seize the raw materials of South-East Asia, in particular, the oil of the Dutch East Indies.

During the closing months of 1941, the USA and Japan tried to negotiate an agreement to end the trade embargo – but the USA, friendly towards China, would not agree to supply Japan with the oil it so badly needed, unless Japan withdrew its forces from the Asian mainland of China, Korea and Manchuria.

General Hideki Tōjō

On 14 October 1941, Army Minister General Hideki Tōjō – a name that would become famous during the war to come – told the Japanese Cabinet that widespread troop withdrawals in China were not acceptable to the military. Retreat would endanger Japan's position in Manchuria, Korea and China. On 16 October, the cabinet resigned, unwilling to launch another war.

The day after the government resigned, 17 October 1941, General Tōjō became the Japanese Prime Minister – he would also continue as War Minister. Essentially, the army had become dictator to Japan – and Tōjō, the army representative, was now Prime Minister.

Both the Japanese army and navy wanted war for their own reasons. The navy was concerned about the diminishing oil reserves; and the army believed that American aid to China would increase and undermine its position there. Japan would pursue the diplomatic negotiations to end the embargo – but only until midnight on 30 November 1941.

At a Japanese Imperial Conference on 1 December 1941, with no end to the embargo agreed, General Tōjō advised that war was necessary to preserve the Japanese Empire. Orders were sent out to military commanders that hostilities would commence on 8 December 1941 (7 December east of the International Date Line).

Japan's war planners hoped to quickly build an empire so large that the Western powers would not be able to countenance the cost of retaking it. She also hoped that her Axis partners in Germany and Italy would prevail over the Soviets and Britain in Europe, and that thereafter, Japan might negotiate peace with an isolated United States. Anti-war rhetoric and political divisions apparent within America encouraged the Japanese in this view. However, the Japanese plan depended to a large degree upon Germany winning in Europe. It was a gamble in which they did not hold all the cards.

The Japanese military knew there was only a limited chance of winning a prolonged war with America, but the move of the US Fleet to Hawaii in the spring of 1940 had opened up the possibility of a pre-emptive knock-out strike. If Japan could destroy the main American offensive weapon – its fleet – in one blow, it might buy enough time to forge a viable Pacific Empire.

Admiral Yamamoto Isoroku

The commander-in-chief of Japan's Combined Fleet, Admiral Yamamoto Isoroku, knew Japan had only a limited chance of winning a prolonged war – but he had a background in naval aviation and the recent success of British carrier-launched biplanes against the Italian Fleet at Taranto on 11 November 1940 had been noted at the time.

Development of a torpedo that could be dropped to run in the shallow waters of Hawaii started. If an attack on Pearl Harbor could be successfully carried out, the 11 battleships and ten aircraft carriers of the Imperial Japanese Navy should be more than a match for remaining Allied naval forces in the area. The Japanese battleships and aircraft carriers could be relied upon to shield the army's invasion convoys as they sailed for South-East Asia.

The gamble was on.

CHAPTER SIX

FORCE Z IS DEPLOYED – ARRIVAL AT SINGAPORE

On 20 October 1941, the Admiralty accepted Churchill's suggestion of sending a small force of two capital ships and an aircraft carrier to Singapore as a deterrent against Japanese expansionist aggression. His power of character had successfully pushed his plan through in preference to the Admiralty's plan to build up a Far East Fleet in the Indian Ocean during 1942. Churchill conceded privately that the creation of a Far Eastern Squadron such as Force Z was as much a political as a naval gesture. Force Z would initially be called 'Force G' whilst en route to Singapore: on arrival, it would be redesignated as 'Force Z'.

Churchill's much beloved and newest battleship, *Prince of Wales*, had, after much debate, been selected to be sent as the main part of Force Z; and he chose Admiral Sir Tom Phillips to command. The *Prince of Wales* was a brand new battleship, barely completed when the *Bismarck* broke out into the North Atlantic in May 1941 to start terrorising Allied shipping. The famous order went out from Churchill that the *Bismarck* should be sunk, and *Prince of Wales* had been pivotal in the action, scoring the crucial hit on *Bismarck* that caused an oil leak and set in motion the chain of events that would lead to her being sent to the bottom.

Doubters about the ability of capital ships to withstand a concentrated air attack had been voicing their concerns since the end of World War I, and famously, the American Brigadier-General Billy Mitchell (assistant chief of the US Army Air Corps between 1919 and 1925) had argued forcibly that aircraft could sink by bomb or torpedo any ship afloat. He proved it in unsatisfactory trials in 1921, during which his aircraft sank two empty ex-German warships: a battleship and a cruiser; and three old American battleships were sunk during trials over the next two years. His views did not gain approval, and as he continued to agitate forcibly, he was exiled to a remote command and then court-martialed and suspended from duty for publishing his views in the press without official permission.

Two decades later, by the outbreak of World War II, the main threat to a capital ship was still seen as the guns of another big ship or torpedo by submarine. Twelve Allied capital ships had been sunk between the opening of the war in September 1939 and the end of November 1941. Most were sunk by gunfire from other big ships, and some, like the unfortunate and elderly *Royal Oak*, at anchor in Scapa Flow, had been torpedoed. It was still felt that a battleship could use her speed to outrun an enemy submarine, and that her waterline armour belt and system of water-tight compartments would keep her safe if struck by a torpedo. Attack by aircraft was still not generally regarded as a particularly significant danger as to date no capital ships had being sunk by air attack in action – although many smaller ships, including five British cruisers and 28 destroyers had been. The British battleships *Barham* and *Warspite* had in fact withstood direct hits by bombs at sea – as had the German ships *Scharnhorst* and *Gneisenau*. In any event, Force Z was to have its own carrier, whose fighter aircraft should be able to protect the force from air attack. Once in Singapore, ground-based RAF fighters would also be able to provide fighter support for Force Z on any sortie – or so the planning went.

Five months after the *Bismarck* action, after moving down from Scapa Flow, *Prince of Wales* left Greenock on 25 October 1941, bound for Singapore via Freetown, Sierra Leone and Cape Town. The E-class destroyers *Electra* and *Express* – modern ships built in the mid 1930s that could make 35 knots and carried 4.7-inch guns – were detached from the Home Fleet to join her. The 1,350-ton H-class destroyer *Hesperus*, built in 1937, would accompany the group (on loan from Western Approaches) for the first part of the voyage; and a fourth destroyer – HMS *Legion* – joined the escorts whilst *Express* and *Electra* went to refuel from a tanker in the Azores. When *Express* and *Electra* returned, *Hesperus* and *Legion* parted company for Gibraltar – their role in Force G was at an end. The J-class destroyer, HMS *Jupiter*, and the E-class destroyer, HMS *Encounter*, were detached from the Mediterranean Fleet with orders to rendezvous with Force G at Colombo in Ceylon.

The modern aircraft carrier, HMS *Indomitable*, which had been launched on 26 March 1940 and only commissioned that October of 1941, was tasked to join Force G to provide air cover for the squadron. She had sailed to the West Indies on her maiden voyage shortly after her launch, but whilst there, on 3 November 1941, had run aground on a coral reef near Kingston, Jamaica, as she went to enter the harbour. She was sent to the Norfolk Navy Yard in the USA for repair, and although the repairs were completed in 12 days and she was returned to service shortly afterwards, she would be unable to reach Singapore in sufficient time to provide air cover for Force Z. When Force Z reached Singapore, *Indomitable* was still undergoing training in the West Indies and no other large carrier was available. The carefully constructed plan had changed just days into the mission – in the most ominous fashion.

On 5 November 1941, 11 days out from Greenock, *Prince of Wales* and her two destroyers put into Freetown in Sierra Leone on the west coast of Africa. This was one of the intermediate refueling points established by the Admiralty, well before the war, as part of their 20-year old plan to allow a battle fleet to sail from home waters to reinforce the Singapore Naval Base if the Mediterranean was blocked to safe passage.

As Force G left Freetown the next day, Sunderland flying boats of 95 Squadron based in Sierra Leone flew anti-submarine patrols until the range became too great. The next port of call for Force G was scheduled to be Cape Town in South Africa, but on the way, heavy seas slowed the group. One crewman on the destroyer *Express* was washed overboard and lost. The two destroyers were forced to slow down by the seas and the much larger *Prince of Wales* went on alone. In Cape Town, *Prince of Wales* took on 39 fresh ratings – most were naval prisoners who had jumped previous ships visiting South Africa. Captain Leach welcomed them aboard and promised them a fresh start.

As Force G left Cape Town, proceeded round the southernmost point of South Africa and moved out into the Indian Ocean, bound for Colombo in Ceylon (modern day Sri Lanka), the battlecruiser *Repulse*, already in the Indian Ocean, was also ordered to Colombo to rendezvous with Force G.

Force Z destroyer HMS Electra

Force G escort destroyer HMS Hesperus

Force Z destroyer HMS Express

After another 10-day steam from Cape Town, which included refueling stops at Mauritius and Gan, *Prince of Wales* and Force G arrived at Colombo. The hot tropical weather was already causing extremes of temperatures below decks and much suffering. Engine room temperatures were recorded as being between 105°F and 122°F, and X & Y action machinery room temperatures were above 150°F when the machines were running for more than four hours.

Repulse arrived at Colombo well ahead of Force G, and as she waited for Force G to arrive she used her time to escort convoys off the East African coast. Although newspapers were officially permitted to report the presence of *Prince of Wales* by name, they were prohibited from referring to *Repulse* by name – she was to be called 'a large warship' in a move designed to conceal from the Japanese the strength and quality of the force about to sail for Singapore.

After the destroyers *Encounter* and *Jupiter* arrived on 29 November 1941, *Prince of Wales* sailed from Colombo, on the west coast of Ceylon, with *Electra*, *Encounter*, *Express*, and *Jupiter*, and *Repulse* left the port of Trincomalee on Ceylon's east coast. Force G gathered at a rendezvous point at sea and, minus the aircraft carrier, set a south-east course for Singapore.

Admiral Sir Tom Phillips (right) and Rear Admiral Arthur Palliser await the arrival of Force G at Singapore Naval Base on 2 December 1941. (IWM)

The day before Force G arrived at Singapore, 1 December 1941, in light of the rapidly growing Japanese threat, a state of emergency was declared in Malaya, and British commanders at Singapore mobilised the Volunteer Forces in Malaya. The RAF started flying daily reconnaissance sorties deep into the Gulf of Siam and the South China Sea. The chief of staff in London advised the commander-in-chief of the British Far East Command covering Singapore, Malaya, Burma and Hong Kong – Air Chief Marshal Sir Henry Robert Moore Brooke-Popham – that he could launch Operation Matador on his own initiative if a Japanese convoy was determined to be sailing for southern Thailand, or if the Japanese attacked any other part of Thai, British or Dutch territory. In Operation Matador, British land-forces would enter southern Thailand to thwart Japanese landings on the eastern coastline. The essence of the strategy was to ensure the landward security of Singapore – the whole of the Malayan mainland had to be held. The Admiralty sent a signal to Admiral Phillips suggesting that either or both of the capital ships should leave Singapore soon after their arrival and cruise in waters east of Singapore, 'to disconcert the Japanese'.

Three days after departing Colombo, on 2 December 1941, Force G arrived at Singapore to much fanfare and flag-waving. In a show of force, the impressive line of ships steamed around the island and up the Johor Strait that separates Singapore Island from mainland Malaya, and entered the naval base. Admiral Sir Tom Phillips, who had gone on ahead of Force G by air, was waiting at the pier-side and watched as *Prince of Wales* berthed. He was the first of the large welcoming party up the gangplank. *Repulse* moored out in the stream to keep her out of easy view of prying eyes, and as it had been decided to keep the exact composition of Force G a secret, once again local newspapers were directed not to refer to her by name and only report the presence of *Prince of Wales*, 'with other heavy ships and auxiliary vessels'. *Prince of Wales* was dry-docked to have her hull cleaned and for her boilers to be cleaned, to maintain their efficiency.

Force Z destroyer HMS Tenedos

Force Z destroyer HMAS Vampire

On Wednesday, 3 December 1941, the Admiralty again signalled Phillips, suggesting that *Prince of Wales* and *Repulse* should get away from Singapore sharpish. Phillips undertook to discuss the situation with the Americans, who had eight destroyers in the Dutch East Indies that could be moved to strengthen Singapore's naval defences. He also advised that he would send *Repulse* on a short visit to Darwin in Australia, and asked if the old battleships *Revenge*, *Royal Sovereign*, *Ramillies*, and *Resolution*, previously ear marked for his fleet, could now be sent to Singapore. *Repulse* set sail for Darwin on 5 December, accompanied by the old 1917 destroyer HMS *Tenedos* and the World War I-era Australian Navy destroyer HMAS *Vampire*.

Little did anyone know that the Japanese had already taken the decision that should no agreement be reached with America by 25 November 1941, they would go to war as soon as possible after 1 December. On 1 December, General Tōjō told an Imperial Conference in Tokyo that there was no alternative to war, as Japan could not keep its dominions in China and Asia and live with the resulting economic embargo. Japan was prepared to take on America, the British Empire and the Dutch. The conference determined that the attacks would start on 8 December (albeit the first attacks would start on 7 December by US and British times according to the International Date Line). There would be five separate operations, against:

1. Pearl Harbor
2. The American airfields at Luzon, the largest island in the Philippines
3. The strategically important islands of Guam, Wake, and the Gilbert Islands
4. Hong Kong
5. Siam, Malaya and Singapore

The plan was breathtaking in its audacity.

CHAPTER SEVEN

8 DECEMBER 1941 – SORTIE

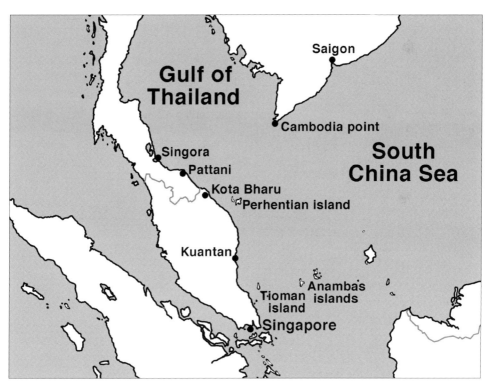

Chart of Malaya and the Gulf of Thailand showing the southern invasion beaches of Singora, Pattani and Kota Bharu

Just two days after Force G's arrival at Singapore, at dawn on 4 December 1941, the first Japanese troop transports bound for Thailand and north-east Malaya left Hainan Island, off the coast of China, for a four-day voyage to the area of operations for the planned assault on 8 December: the small Thai fishing port of Singora on the north-east coast of the

Kra Isthmus, north of Malaya. Nineteen troop transports carried the Japanese Southern Expeditionary Army, made up of 5 Division, 5 Tank Regiment of 25 Army, 41 Regiment and 9 Brigade. An escort of cruisers and destroyers shielded the slow and vulnerable transports. This force would rendezvous on 7 December in the Gulf of Thailand (Siam) with a second convoy of nine further transports, which would set off to the rendezvous point from Saigon and other ports throughout 5 December until 7 December.

The convoys would be protected by two old World War I-era capital ships: the battlecruiser *Kongō* (ironically designed and built by Britain when the two countries had been friendly) and the battleship *Haruna*; along with the 7th Cruiser Squadron and ten submarines deployed in a patrol line. The arrival of *Prince of Wales* and another heavy ship (*Repulse*) had been well heralded by the British, as they implemented their hoped-for deterrent strategy. As a consequence, the Japanese had sent two minelayers to lay 1,000 mines between Tioman Island and the Anambas Islands – directly across the prospective route the British naval squadron would take if they put to sea to attack the Japanese convoys. The Japanese greatly feared what would transpire if the British ships came out and attacked the invasion transports on their way to the beaches. Protected only by one old World War I battleship, a World War I battlecruiser, and the smaller cruisers, the British ships could decimate the invasion force before it even reached the assault beaches.

A total of 26,640 soldiers crammed into the 19 troop transports of the first wave of ships deployed from Hainan Island, off China. These troop transports would sail close to the coast of Indochina to avoid detection for their four-day journey south towards Singora. The Japanese were relying on the bad weather of the breaking monsoon to shield the convoys from British reconnaissance aircraft. They knew that if the invasion forces were spotted and intercepted, the invasion would be in trouble from the start.

The bad weather did indeed prevent British reconnaissance aircraft from flying on 4 December, and only limited flights were possible the following day, 5 December. But on 6 December, for the first time in three days, twin-engine Hudson bombers of No 1 Squadron Royal Australian Air Force took off early in the morning from a rain-swept Kota Bharu air base situated at the every north-easternmost part of the Malayan Peninsula, near the Thailand border. They were tasked to carry out a reconnaissance sweep 185 miles across the Gulf of Siam (Gulf of Thailand) to Cambodia Point.

About midday, the flight spotted three Japanese troop transports and a cruiser steaming south-west around Cambodia Point into the Gulf of Siam. Shortly afterwards, the main Japanese convoy of almost 20 transports was sighted. The Australian planes bravely flew up and down the convoy at a height of less than 1,000 feet, scrutinizing the invasion fleet below. The convoy launched a seaplane, but with enough seen, the Australian planes withdrew into the clouds and radioed the discovery of the invasion fleet back to their base.

When the news subsequently reached British commanders in Singapore, there was, at first, a reluctance to launch Operation Matador straight away. Many still did not believe that war was inevitable and Operation Matador was a politically sensitive operation, as it involved violating Thailand's neutrality by invading its territory. There was still doubt about the convoy's destination and some feared the convoy might simply be a trick to entice Britain to implement Operation Matador by invading Thailand first. *Repulse*, however, was recalled from her voyage to Darwin.

Whilst British commanders assessed the situation and tried to work out what to do, the next day, 7 December 1941, very heavy weather closed in again with rain-squalls, fog, and dense cloud reducing visibility for reconnaissance aircraft.

Just after 9 a.m., on 7 December 1941, the now-combined Japanese invasion convoy split into several smaller sections: one bound for Kota Bharu in north-eastern Malaya; one for the southern Thai towns of Singora and Pattani near the Malayan border; and the others for destinations further north in Thailand. Later that morning, Japanese aircraft providing air cover for the convoy shot down a RAF Catalina flying-boat, before it could radio back to base about Japanese ship movements. During the afternoon, RAF planes spotted Japanese ships closing on Singora, but this information did not reach British HQ at Singapore until 9 p.m., that night. It was now clearly too late to launch Operation Matador – British commanders had delayed too long. There was much relief when *Repulse* and her two escort destroyers arrived back at Singapore after a high-speed run.

As British commanders at Singapore tried to decide how to deal with the Japanese naval movements towards the Thai and northern Malayan coast, other Japanese fleets were moving out across the Pacific towards the other four targets: Pearl Harbor; the American airfields at Luzon in the Philippines; Guam and the Wake and Gilbert Islands; and the other great bastion of British colonial power, Hong Kong.

A powerful fleet of six Japanese aircraft carriers and support ships had in fact also put to sea almost two weeks earlier, on 26 November 1941, under the command of Admiral Nagumo – and had sailed across the Pacific in total secrecy towards Hawaii.

Early on Sunday 7 December, 183 Japanese aircraft were launched from these carriers for the now infamous raid on Pearl Harbor. Just after 7 a.m., an American radar-operator in Hawaii spotted a huge flight of aircraft to the north on his screen. Alerting his superior, he was told that the planes were American B-17s en route from California. There was no coordinated system of American aerial reconnaissance in place at this time.

Admiral Chūichi Nagumo

Just after 8 a.m., the first wave of Japanese bombers and fighters swept across Pearl Harbor, taking everyone there by complete surprise. Some Japanese aircraft headed for the military airfields, where hundreds of largely unprotected US planes were neatly lined up in rows. A second wave of Japanese aircraft followed at 8.45 a.m.

The largest Japanese group attacked US Pacific Fleet warships lined up in Battleship Row. The battleship USS *Arizona* exploded from a bomb hit at the forward magazine, killing 1,177 officers and men. There were 429 men trapped inside the battleship USS *Oklahoma*, as it capsized after flooding caused by torpedo strikes. The battleship USS *West Virginia* was engulfed in flames, and the battleship USS *California* sank and settled on the bottom in shallow water. The other four battleships in the port were all damaged, with the crippled USS *Nevada* being successfully beached. By the time the assault was over, eight battleships and many smaller vessels were sunk or badly damaged. A total of 2,403 Americans had been killed and 1,178 wounded.

Although a stunning tactical success for the Japanese, strategically the attack was less significant. The vast fuel dumps for the Pacific Fleet had not been damaged and the powerful American aircraft carriers, which had been away at sea that day, had not been located or damaged. Instead of launching a third wave to destroy the American fuel dumps and vital repair facilities, which would have rendered the whole base at Hawaii useless, and rather than hunting down the now vulnerable American carriers, Admiral Nagumo withdrew his fleet to safety. Hawaii remained a powerful naval base: a submarine and intelligence base which was later instrumental in Japan's defeat. Rather than crippling American naval power in the Pacific long enough to allow Japan to secure her position, the raid had left Hawaii – and American naval power in the Pacific – largely intact. Worse still for the Japanese, it now brought America into the war in the Pacific and Asia.

Japanese forces had also gathered for an immediate assault on British Hong Kong, which had only a garrison of six battalions, artillery and some volunteer units. As the siege of Hong Kong Island began, the small garrison was not expected to hold out long.

In the Philippines, despite intelligence having been passed to American forces about the raid on Pearl Harbor, the US Army Air Force was still caught by surprise. Japanese carrier-launched aircraft swooped in from the sea on the opening day to find US bombers and fighters parked wing to wing in neat rows at their air bases, and many were destroyed on the ground with the opening attacks. Simultaneously, Japanese troops were landing at several points along the Philippine coastline.

Off southern Thailand, at about 2.20 a.m., on 8 December 1941 – not long after the start of the Pearl Harbor raid – the main Japanese convoy anchored off Singora, just north of the Malay border with Thailand. Japanese assault troops went ashore by landing craft, and the light Thai resistance ended after just a few hours.

At 3.30 a.m., radar stations far to the south at Singapore picked up unidentified aircraft 140 miles away to the north. Just after 4 a.m., Japanese twin-engine bombers, which had flown all the way from Indochina, roared across the Singapore night, guided by the bright lights of the city. The Air Raid Precautions HQ was un-manned and no warning could be passed to the civilian authorities to initiate a black out.

Almost 200 casualties were caused by Japanese bombs dropped on Singapore that night – and two of the island's RAF aerodromes were also bombed. At another airfield, three RAF

Brewster F2A Buffalo fighter aircraft stood ready to take to the skies to attack the Japanese long-range bombers, but they were refused permission to take off for fear of being hit by British anti-aircraft fire. As dawn the next morning arrived, disbelieving crowds gathered in the city to inspect the bomb craters. The Japanese population in Malaya was swiftly rounded up and interned by the British.

The section of the Japanese invasion force bound for Kota Bharu (on the north-east Malayan coastline) was carrying 5,300 soldiers in large troop transports. They arrived and anchored before midnight on 7 / 8 December – the landing timed to coincide with the raid on Pearl Harbor. The strategic target for the Japanese was the RAF Kota Bharu airfield, which was located halfway between the town and the invasion beach. Troops ashore spotted the silhouettes of the large Japanese troop transports looming offshore in the darkness, and a few minutes later they were being shelled.

At 12.45 a.m., armour-plated barges packed with Japanese assault troops were lowered from the transports and started to head towards the shore. News of the invasion at Kota Bharu reached British command in Singapore at about 1 a.m.

Ashore, British 18-pounder guns on the beach started firing at the dark ships at sea. Pillboxes had been built at 1,000-yard intervals along the shore, and these also opened up with a withering fire on the assault barges, with several being quickly sunk or badly damaged.

Once the barges reached the shore, the first Japanese assault troops took heavy casualties as they landed and tried to force a passage through the barbed wire that lined the beaches. Several barges, however, managed to motor up a creek mouth that opened into an inlet behind the ends of the beaches – and behind the beach defences. Attacked now from front and behind, the pillboxes either side of the creek were soon captured and Japanese troops advanced along the beach in both directions. Soon they had control of a 2,000-yard-long strip.

The Japanese had to quickly gain control of the British airfield at Kota Bharu some 2 miles inland – where shocked aircrew could hear the sound of gunfire carrying from the beaches. The Japanese needed to quickly neutralize the threat its planes posed to the beach assault troops and vulnerable static troop transports offshore. News of the landing quickly reached the airfield and Hudson bombers of No 1 Squadron RAAF began taking off at 2–3-minute intervals. Once airborne, it was but a short hop before they were in night-combat, swooping in to attack the Japanese ships and barges, almost at mast-top height. Deadly Japanese anti-aircraft fire from the ships soon took its toll, with one Hudson bomber being shot down and crashing into a barge.

RAAF bombing soon set the Japanese transport *Awagisan Maru* on fire from stem to stern – she was later abandoned and sank. Several hits were also scored on the two other troop transports, and the aerial assault badly disrupted the disembarkation of the third and final wave of infantry.

But despite these losses, the Japanese fought tenaciously and brutally, and by daybreak they had firmly established themselves in their beach bridgehead. As Commonwealth forces struggled to contain them, two reserve battalions were ordered to counter-attack and attempt to push the Japanese back into the sea. However, the two reserve battalions struggled in many places to get through the jungle, deep swollen streams, and islands with thick undergrowth behind the beaches, to join with the enemy.

RAF Bristol Blenheim light bombers

As the dawn of 8 December broke in Singapore, British commanders were well briefed on the Kota Bharu landing, but were waiting for the results of RAF reconnaissance flights to Singora, further to the north, in Thailand. By 9.45 a.m., news of a mass of Japanese shipping at Singora reached the British commander-in-chief, who finally cancelled Operation Matador. It had clearly been superceded by events – the Japanese had won the race for Singora and the forward defence of Malaya and Singapore was already in disarray.

At 6.30 a.m., the Hudson bombers of No 8 Squadron RAAF and the Blenheims of No. 60 Squadron RAF left Kuantan airfield, situated halfway down the Malay Peninsula, to attack the Japanese landing-force further north at Kota Bharu. Arriving over the landing area, they bombed the already disabled transport ships as well as the assault barges crowding the shore. Aircraft from other RAF squadrons in Malaya arrived overhead and joined the fray.

Japanese bombers arrived above Kota Bharu soon after 9 a.m., for the first attacks on the vital British airfield there. By late afternoon, Japanese ground-troops had pushed off the beach and reached the airfield boundary 2 miles inshore. Permission was given for the airfield to be evacuated.

Later in the day, at 6 p.m., Major General Barstow, in charge of the 9th Indian Division at Kota Bharu, was advised that he could retire from Kota Bharu at his own discretion and that he should not risk the annihilation of his command. With the RAF airfield there now abandoned, there was no reason for his isolated division to remain at Kota Bharu – its purpose had been to defend the airfield, not the town. The division withdrew to a new line 4–5 miles inland, and the petrol dump at Kota Bharu was set alight by British artillery fire to prevent it falling to the Japanese.

In the inky darkness of a rain-swept Malayan night, across flooded streams and swamps and continually harassed by Japanese patrols, the 9th Indian Division retreated inland. With the coming of the dawn of 9 December 1941, sporadic skirmishes were breaking out as the Japanese started to outflank the retreating division. Over the next two days, the Indian troops were forced to withdraw almost 30 miles inland from the invasion beaches.

At the Sungei Petani airfield to the north-west of the Malay Peninsula, two RAF Brewster Buffalo fighters managed to get into the air, but as they closed on the Japanese aircraft swooping in to attack the airfield, they found their guns had no ammunition loaded. Ten Buffalo fighters and Blenheim light bombers were damaged on the ground by phosphorus-charged incendiary bombs.

At the north-west Malayan Alor Setar RAF base, nine Blenheim bombers were also caught and destroyed or damaged on the ground, along with the base's buildings, and the fuel dump was set ablaze. The remaining aircraft that could fly at these two RAF northern bases were ordered back to a safer southern airfield, but by the end of 8 December, the RAF in northern Malaya had lost over half its flying strength – yet it still faced 400–500 Japanese aircraft based in Indochina. It had been a disastrous day for the RAF.

In Singapore, HMS *Repulse* had returned on 7 December at speed from her deployment to Darwin, and the crew of *Prince of Wales* readied the great ship for sea, patching up unfinished engineering repairs. As the Japanese landings at Kota Bharu were taking place on the night of 7 / 8 December, the British capital ships were still in Singapore Naval Base.

Many have queried how the landings would have gone if Force Z had been sent to sea during the night of 6 / 7 December after the first reports came in of a Japanese fleet heading for the Gulf of Siam. Would the outcome have been different? The approach of the undoubted might of Force Z might have caused the Japanese to divert the landing at Kota Bharu to Singora. If not, Force Z might have been able to raid the Japanese transports and decimate the invasion ships off Kota Bharu – and the landing may have been thwarted. Alternatively, Force Z might have been able to intercept the convoys heading for Singora and Pattani. Either way, by 8 December, Force Z had missed the opportunity to launch a significant strike against the Japanese invasion of Thailand and northern Malaya.

In Singapore, on the morning of 8 December, faced with reports of the Japanese landings to the north, Admiral Phillips reviewed all the ships available to him and determined that he would take *Prince of Wales*, *Repulse* and four destroyers – *Express*, *Electra*, *Tenedos*, and *Vampire* – to sea later that evening, 8 December. The force – now designated Force Z – would sortie northwards to attack Japanese troops and shipping at Singora, after first light on 10 December. An evening departure was chosen to conceal the sailing from possible Japanese agents on Singapore. For the capital ships to remain at Singapore was unwise, as the night bombing of Singapore had shown that the naval base was already vulnerable to bombing – the navy also could not head south and leave the army and Malaya unsupported. Phillips took a calculated risk in sortie-ing Force Z – intending only to go through with his plan if Force Z remained unsighted during the run north on 9 December. He hoped that the monsoon rains and low cloud would shield Force Z from observation.

Phillips did not fear high-level bombing or dive-bombers, as he believed that his ships' anti-aircraft fire could deal with those threats – but he was concerned about attack by torpedo-bombers. However, he believed that if Force Z could achieve total surprise, the Japanese aircraft operating at Singora available to attack Force Z would be armed for land operations, and would not be carrying anti-ship bombs and torpedoes. As Force Z returned to Singapore, after a successful attack at Singora, he felt his ships would face only hastily-organized bombers flying from Indochina, well to the north.

At the time, British military thinking – based on the capabilities of their own torpedo-carrying aircraft – accepted that the risk of aerial torpedo attack within 200 miles of enemy airfields was great. But the risk of aerial torpedo attack was believed to decrease to almost zero at a range of 400 miles – the limit of their conventional torpedo-bombers. British intelligence at the time had no idea that the Japanese twin-engine bombers which had flown 600 miles from Indochina for the bombing raid on Singapore the night before could be easily re-armed as torpedo-bombers. Their range in fact was 1,000 miles.

It was felt impossible for the Royal Navy not to attempt to assist whilst the army and RAF were being driven back on the land. The plan for a sudden naval raid, though undoubtedly hazardous, was thought acceptable. The psychological effect of Force Z putting to sea on both the Japanese and British was also taken into account. It could strike fear into the Japanese and paralyse their movements; and it would bolster British morale. But many British officers secretly had their doubts about the plan.

Phillips was very conscious that Force Z did not have the planned aircraft carrier, but with RAF airfields scattered all across Malaya, he felt air-cover should be possible. Accordingly, on the morning of 8 December, before Kota Bharu airbase had been abandoned and before the disastrous day had unfolded for the RAF across Malaya, Phillips had requested that the RAF provide air reconnaissance ahead of Force Z. He also asked for fighter protection off Singora (120 nautical miles further north of Kota Bharu) after dawn on 10 December. Phillips met with the RAF air vice-marshal in charge, to discuss how this should be organised later in the morning.

But by the afternoon of 8 December 1941, in light of the disaster unfolding for the RAF across northern Malaya and the need to maintain Singapore's own air defences, Phillips was advised that whilst aerial reconnaissance was possible, fighter protection off Singora on 10 December was unlikely. Of the four squadrons of Buffalo fighter aircraft at Singapore, only one squadron was allocated to defence of the Royal Navy vessels. The protection of Force Z came only as a third priority for the RAF – behind the battle in northern Malaya and the air defence of Singapore.

The commander of 453 Squadron, which was earmarked by the RAF as fleet-defence squadron, met Phillips' air liaison officer and offered to put in place a flight-roster using the east coast of Malaya airfields, which would allow a standing patrol of six aircraft above Force Z at all times in daylight. But this scheme required Force Z to sail close to the Malayan coast – no further than 60 miles from the coast at any time, and not more than 100 miles north of Kota Bharu. Admiral Phillips felt he could not accept these conditions which would restrict his freedom to operate Force Z as required. There was the Japanese minefield to consider, and additionally, Phillips wasn't prepared to agree to any breaking of radio silence for his ships (which would be required for such naval/airforce cooperation), as that could lead to the discovery of Force Z's location. To preserve secrecy and retain the essential element of surprise, radio silence would be strictly maintained by Force Z at sea. Phillips also could not agree to Force Z staying close to the shore, as persons ashore and in the immediate coastal waters would see the force and perhaps give away its location to Japanese forces. No workable arrangement could be found between the RAF and the Royal Navy. Admiral Sir Tom Phillips knew that he could not have or expect shore-based air cover but resolved to take a calculated risk and sortie Force Z. His powerful squadron could outrun any Japanese submarine and stand up to any of the Japanese warships known to be in the area. He could steer clear of the area where mines were believed to have been laid. The risk of torpedo bomber attack was not understood.

The fleet-defence Buffalo fighters at Singapore were, however, kept at the disposal of the navy, at constant daylight readiness, should Force Z be attacked and call for help.

Force Z left Singapore for the open South China Sea on 8 December 1941. The destroyer *Vampire* was first away at 5.10 p.m., followed by the other destroyer *Tenedos*, then *Repulse*, and lastly, *Prince of Wales*. The destroyers *Electra* and *Express* had been at sea that day exercising their mine sweeping gear and would rendezvous outside the anti-submarine boom-nets off Changi point. There were three old cruisers also berthed at Singapore – but only one of was ready to sail and Phillips decided to leave her behind.

Force Z would keep clear of the area where Intelligence believed mines had been laid, and the fast ships of the squadron could outrun any submarine or old Japanese battleship. If Force Z could preserve the element of surprise and get into the right position, the big guns of *Prince of Wales* and *Repulse* could inflict a stunning slaughter upon the Japanese ships off the invasion beaches and the Japanese troops already ashore. If this could be pulled off, it would be a great victory for the Royal Navy. As Force Z left Singapore harbour, no capital ship had ever been sunk by air attack in action whilst at sea.

Once clear of the land, Force Z formed up into its night-cruising formation for the first night at sea. *Prince of Wales* overtook *Repulse*, which followed on 800 yards astern of the flagship. *Express* moved ahead to take up a position well in front of the squadron and streamed out her high-speed mine-sweeping gear. The six warships steamed off into the pitch darkness of a tropical night at 17.5 knots. *Electra* took over the lead when *Express's* mine-sweeping gear failed.

HMS Repulse *sorties from Singapore with Force Z on 8 December 1941. (IWM)*

HMS Prince of Wales *sorties from Singapore with Force Z on 8 December 1941. (IWM)*

Force Z initially sailed well to the north-east, away from the land, to avoid detection and to avoid the Japanese minefield between Tioman Island and the Anambas Islands. The force rounded the east side of the Anambas Islands before turning their bows in the darkness of night to the north. The mighty ships then set a course for the Gulf of Siam, as they headed into the open expanse of the South China Sea.

Eight hours after sailing however, a signal from Rear Admiral Palliser in Singapore was received in *Prince of Wales*. The RAF had been pulverised in the north of Malaya and although reconnaisance by one Catalina seaplane would be provided from the 9 December onwards, it was stressed that fighter protection on 10 December off Singora would not be possible.

As dawn broke the following day, 9 December 1941, the conditions were perfect for Force Z – it was rainy and cloudy and offered good protection from Japanese air reconnaissance. Classic monsoon conditions prevailed, reducing visibility to half a mile. The die was cast.

CHAPTER EIGHT

10 DECEMBER 1941 – THE BATTLE

At 1.45 p.m., on 9 December 1941 – the day after Force Z left Singapore – unknown to the British squadron, the Japanese submarine *I-65* spotted the two capital ships and shadowed them for over three hours, reporting back the presence of 'two enemy battleships' (*sic*). Force Z was so distant that the four much smaller escort destroyers were not spotted.

Later that afternoon, at about 4.45 p.m., with only just over an hour to go until sunset ushered in its dark cloak of invisibility (at a few minutes after 6 p.m.), the skies ominously cleared and three Japanese aircraft were spotted. These were seaplanes from Japanese scouting cruisers and they shadowed Force Z until dark. In a brief period of clear skies, between the monsoon cloak of invisibility being lifted and the darkness of night, Force Z had been compromised. RAF fighters from a carrier (or land-based) would have been extremely helpful at this point, by driving the Japanese seaplanes away and allowing Force Z to alter course unobserved and escape south. But the only Allied aircraft seen that evening was the single RAF Catalina flying-boat on reconnaisance patrol.

Phillips was aware that with Force Z now spotted by Japanese aircraft, the prospect of a punishing surprise attack at Kota Bharu or Singora had been lost. The sortie so far had been a great disappointment, as no Japanese shipping at all had been encountered (the Japanese convoys had in fact reached Singora two days earlier).

Phillips had Force Z maintain its northerly course until darkness fell and he was sure that the shadowing aircraft had departed. The old World War I-era destroyer *Tenedos* had played her role as escort well, but she had a limited fuel capacity and Phillips thought she might become a liability in the event of a high-speed chase back to Singapore. At 6.30 p.m., after darkness had fallen, he ordered her to turn back towards Singapore and passed a signal to her to be transmitted by the destroyer to Singapore command at 8 a.m. the next morning. This signal requested that as many destroyers as possible – including the American destroyers that were expected soon at Singapore – should come out to meet Force Z on its return just north of the Anambas Islands, at dawn on 11 December. The two capital ships could then be escorted past any Japanese submarines that might be lying in wait there. Although Force Z had been spotted, now that it was cloaked in darkness Phillips decided against aborting the mission and returning to Singapore.

At 6.55 p.m. – half an hour after *Tenedos* had departed and with no sign of other Japanese reconnaissance aircraft – Phillips ordered Force Z to steer north-west, and speed was worked up to 26 knots towards the northern invasion beaches, into the very heart of enemy-dominated waters.

Within only a few minutes, however, lookouts on *Electra* sighted a flare, believed to be about 5 miles ahead. At 7.30 p.m., Phillips ordered all ships to turn to port in order to pass well clear of the flare's position. Force Z was now almost 300 miles north of Singapore.

Just then, a signal arrived from Singapore command reporting that one Japanese battleship, an M-class cruiser, 11 destroyers and a number of transports had been spotted close to the coast between Kota Bharu and Perhentian Island by air reconnaissance that afternoon. This was the long-awaited signal Phillips had hoped for, giving him the latest news about the Japanese landing-areas. A further signal reported the time of the Intelligence as being 10.30 a.m. that morning. Kota Bharu was 130 miles further south towards Singapore than Singora – a diversion to Kota Bharu would be far less hazardous for the ships of Force Z when daylight came. (The signal however did not advise that since the air reconnaissance that morning, the Japanese had almost completed their landings at Kota Bharu and most of the ships involved were either on their way back to Indochina or hunting for Force Z itself.)

Phillips was unaware that, in the darkness, Force Z had actually closed to within 5 miles of the Japanese cruisers and destroyers which were protecting the invasion of Thailand and Malaya. The flare had been at their location. If Force Z continued northwards for perhaps as little as less than an hour, they might have contacted the light Japanese naval forces at a time when the two Japanese capital ships were still well to the north. The Japanese had deliberately sortied their cruisers to the south, and were freely using their radios in an attempt to lure the British into battle – they wanted to draw the British squadron northwards for a fight the following morning. Orders had already given for all available Japanese warships to head towards the reported location of Force Z, to search for and contact the British squadron. Force Z may have been out hunting, but unknowingly, she herself was also being hunted.

Eleven land-based Mitsubishi bombers from Saigon were tasked to search for Force Z after dark. One Mitsubishi spotted two bright lanes of white foam in the darkness – the slightly phosphorescent wakes of the two British capital ships. He flew carefully along the wakes and soon came up behind the black silhouettes of the British ships. He climbed away and radioed a sighting report.

Japanese Mitsubishi 'Nell' bombers

When the first reports of Force Z's location had come through, 53 additional torpedo- and bomb-carrying aircraft – the main attack force – had taken off from Saigon. They now reached the area, but at first they were unable to locate Force Z due to poor weather and bad visibility. But then, one bomber sighted ships below in the darkness – and assumed it was Force Z. A flare was dropped and the plane then put out a radio transmission confirming that a flare had been dropped and directing other aircraft to the area. This radio report caused great consternation on the Japanese flagship *Chokai* – as it was this ship that had been misidentified below and was now being illuminated by the flare. This was the flare spotted on *Electra* at 7.30 p.m. and thought to be about 5 miles ahead. Neither side knew just how close the two naval forces had been. If there had been no flare the two sides would have run into each other. How might the course of history have been changed?

Back in Saigon, Japanese command realised the confusion that was being wrought by the uncoordinated night-hunt for Force Z, and ordered the air search to be discontinued. The 53 bombers were ordered back to base. Japanese surface commanders were deeply worried about a naval engagement with the British in poor visibility, as the British ships were believed to be equipped with a new invention: radar-controlled guns capable of zeroing in on a distant enemy in darkness. The Japanese ships were at a great disadvantage and they knew that the14 and 15-inch guns and the armour of the two British capital ships was vastly superior to their 8-inch cruiser guns and light armour. As with British naval thinking, not everyone in the Japanese Navy believed that a battleship could be sunk by air attack at this time. They knew *Prince of Wales* was present – and they knew she was the latest type of allegedly unsinkable battleship.

When Force Z turned to port to avoid the area where the flare had been seen, although most on the British ships expected the northerly course to be resumed soon afterwards, Admiral Sir Tom Phillips had to take a tough decision. He knew from the earlier signal that RAF fighter cover over Singora 130 miles to the north of Kota Bharu was no longer available. He knew Force Z had been spotted and that he had lost the vital element of surprise – and that, come the morning, there would be Japanese aircraft and warships all around him. He also knew that with the discovery of Force Z, the Japanese would have scattered all their vulnerable merchant ships and transports: the waters off Singora and Kota Bharu would be empty of easy prey, even if *Repulse* and *Prince of Wales* could fight their way through. He could not risk losing the two capital ships – they were Britain's only significant naval presence in the Far East. There was only one conclusion he could come to as a high-ranking professional naval officer: there was no longer any chance of success. The operation must be called off – and immediately, as they had already lost two valuable hours of darkness when Force Z could have been heading back to Singapore. The original course was never resumed. At 8.05 p.m., a reduction in speed to 20 knots was ordered, and 15 minutes later a new course was given which would take Force Z back to Singapore via the Anambas Islands.

The RAF in Malaya

On 9 December 1941, as Force Z steamed north from Singapore, on land the RAF were again having a torrid time, and a sequence of events now unfolded which would have a critical effect on Force Z. With Kota Bharu airfield up beside the Thailand border now in Japanese hands, the Japanese turned their attention to Kuantan, which lies halfway down the Malayan coast towards Singapore. Like the northern Malayan airfields, it lacked anti-aircraft guns and radar.

About noon on 9 December, with little prior warning to RAF ground staff, Japanese bombers heavily bombed Kuantan airfield from 5,000 feet. After completing their bombing runs, the bombers swooped down and strafed the airfield from a low altitude. Another wave of bombers soon followed and a number of British aircraft were destroyed or damaged on the ground.

With Kuantan airfield under heavy attack, RAF Air Headquarters Singapore decided to withdraw all British aircraft from Kuantan to Singapore. By 4 p.m., all the aircraft had left. Their departure sparked rumours that an evacuation of all personnel had been ordered, though this was not the case. The mainly Australian ground staff seized any transport they could find and fled inland to the nearest railway station, leaving only a handful of men and the stunned station commander at the airfield. Elsewhere, three of six RAF Blenheim bombers sent to bomb Singora airfield, which the Japanese were now using, were shot down.

Japanese bombers raided the RAF aerodrome at Butterworth in the afternoon, and Japanese fighters shot down four British Brewster Buffalo fighters already in the air. A group of Blenheim bombers had been in the process of taking off from Butterworth for another attack on Singora airfield when the Japanese aircraft swooped in. Only two of the Blenheims getting ready to take off actually managed to get airborne – one of which had to return to the airfield. The other Blenheim successfully made it to Singora and dropped its bombs over the airfield.

With the buildings at Butterworth demolished and the fields littered with damaged aircraft, those aircraft that could still fly were ordered to evacuate southwards to Ipoh, Taiping or Singapore.

By the end of 9 December, as Force Z was spotted and went on into the darkness, the RAF in Malaya had been devastated. There were only a few RAF aircraft left in the whole of the Malayan mainland, whilst an estimated 150 Japanese aircraft had already been stationed at Singora and Pattani.

Meanwhile, back at sea, shortly after turning Force Z south towards Singapore at 9.45 p.m., British command in Singapore signalled to Admiral Phillips news of the RAF's disastrous day. They advised Phillips that Kota Bharu airfield had been taken by the Japanese, but that landings were continuing there, and that all the northern aerodromes were becoming untenable. Force Z continued south towards Singapore.

Kuantan

As the five ships of Force Z steamed south towards Singapore, just before midnight on 9–10 December, another brief signal was received:

> 'IMMEDIATE
> ENEMY REPORTED LANDING KUANTAN. LATITUDE 03.50 NORTH.'

Kuantan was a militarily-important coastal town halfway down the Malayan Peninsula, and well south of Force Z's current location. A successful landing there could cut off British troops in northern Malaya. As Kuantan was not far from Force Z's path back to Singapore, Phillips ordered a course-change to proceed to that area to investigate – hoping that the British ships could suddenly appear off Kuantan within five hours (early the next morning) and catch Japanese forces by surprise. Phillips believed Force Z had not been spotted since turning to the south and that the Japanese would still expect them to be heading north. Kuantan was 400 miles from Japanese airfields in Indochina, and he possibly believed that was a safe distance from the Japanese torpedo-bombers based in Saigon. Force Z turned towards Kuantan and speed was increased to 25 knots. The hunt was on again.

Force Z was still maintaining strict radio silence: to break radio silence could let the Japanese know their whereabouts. Signals between the ships were passed by signal lamps. Observing strict radio silence, no radio signal was sent to Singapore command to advise that Force Z was deviating from the route home to Singapore. Naval command in Singapore now had no idea where Force Z was – Force Z had just gone off the map. Had Singapore command been aware of the diversion, then the Fleet Defence Buffalo fighters at Singapore, earmarked for the support of Force Z and kept out of all other fighting, could have been sent to patrol the area the next morning. But the next morning the Buffaloes remained parked on the ground at Singapore.

As the Japanese developed their air and sea search for Force Z, their submarines in patrol lanes further south were ordered to move north and spread out. The old 1925 submarine *I-58* had been running on the surface when, at 11.52 p.m., her lookouts spotted the dark shadows of two large ships only 600 metres away. *I-58* immediately dived and made ready to attack, but as *Prince of Wales* passed by, one of the torpedo-tube hatches jammed. As the crew struggled with the hatch, *Prince of Wales* moved out of range. *Repulse* was following on behind, but by the time the faulty hatch had been cleared only the stern of *Repulse* was visible. Five torpedoes were fired, but all missed. The British force steamed away into the night, oblivious to the attack and not having detected the submarine on the surface with their radar, or whilst it was submerged with ASDIC.

After Force Z passed by, the slow, old submarine surfaced and for five hours struggled to retain contact with the far faster British force, transmitting sighting reports.

At 5 a.m., en route to Kuantan as dawn approached, Force Z went to: 'Full Action Stations'. It was cool and the light spread from the horizon behind the ships to usher in a clear day with excellent visibility. Lookouts scanning the horizon and sky reported no contact in any direction.

A short while later, at 5.15 a.m., four dots were seen on the horizon to the north – at first judged to be a cruiser and three destroyers. Admiral Phillips ordered Force Z to turn towards this sighting, but within minutes the contacts were identified as a trawler towing three barges. The contact was judged not worthy of further investigation and Force Z resumed heading towards Kuantan.

Ominously, at 6.30 a.m., an aircraft, believed to be Japanese, was spotted. It shadowed Force Z for half an hour – the implications were enormous. Force Z had again been spotted – but no action was taken. Radio silence was still maintained and no RAF fighter cover was requested. Force Z sped through the sea towards Kuantan, eager to surprise Japanese shipping in the area.

Once the aircraft had disappeared, the Walrus seaplane aboard *Prince of Wales* was hauled onto its catapult and prepared for a reconnaissance flight ahead of Force Z, to inspect the beaches and harbour at Kuantan. It was to report the situation back to *Prince of Wales* and then fly to Singapore or a friendly airfield to land. It would be too hazardous to stop *Prince of Wales* to recover the seaplane – this would make her vulnerable to submarine attack. At 7.18 a.m., the seaplane was catapulted off the battleship and was soon over Kuantan. A report came back that no Japanese ships could be seen.

By 8 a.m. on 10 December, Force Z itself had arrived offshore from Kuantan. *Prince of Wales* and *Repulse* could not make themselves vulnerable to land-based artillery by approaching too close to land, so they turned to steam parallel to the coast at 15 knots. The destroyer *Express* was detached from the squadron and sent close inshore to reconnoitre. This caused some consternation amongst the crews of the other Force Z ships, as there was nothing unusual to be seen ashore. *Express* seemed to be being sent to confirm what the Walrus seaplane had already found. Force Z, its location now known to the enemy, was being delayed on its return to safety. *Express* soon reported back: 'All is as quiet as a wet Sunday afternoon.' She rejoined Force Z at 8.45 a.m.

Phillips now decided that instead of continuing south towards Singapore, he would turn Force Z north-east to investigate the tug and barges seen nearby earlier. This delay caused even greater concern amongst the crews who were aware they had little surface support from the three remaining destroyers – and no air cover. Force Z appeared to be nonchalantly meandering about, whilst they were sitting ducks for submarine or air attack. A battleship, a battlecruiser and three destroyers now set out to examine one trawler and three barges – a task that one destroyer could have handled speedily. Force Z was by now 450 miles from the Japanese airfields in Indochina, and Phillips may well have believed (based on the short range of British torpedo-bombers) that his ships were beyond the effective range of Japanese torpedo-bombers. He could have possibly assumed that the barges, if Japanese, might be the fore-runners of a larger Japanese force which his big guns could then smash.

The tug and barges were located and discovered to be civilian. The diversion had taken up an hour and a half, and as the search of the vessels neared completion, a Japanese scout plane was seen in the distance. At 10.10 a.m., the calm of the morning was badly shaken when a signal was received from the detached destroyer *Tenedos* – she was being bombed by Japanese aircraft 140 miles south-east of Force Z's current position. If the Japanese could reach *Tenedos*, they could certainly reach Force Z.

When Admiral Kondo, in charge of the Japanese naval force, received *I-58*'s first report just before midnight, he had ordered his cruisers and the two old battleships to give chase. They headed south at 24 knots, but even with an increase in speed after dawn to 28 knots, he realised that his ships would never catch Force Z before they made it back to Singapore. Half an hour after ordering his ships to 28 knots, he abandoned the chase and ordered his ships to turn back to the north. With the surface ships out of the fray, all hope of a strike against the British naval force rested on an air attack.

Air search and the attack on HMS *Tenedos*

Nine Japanese Nell reconnaissance aircraft took off from Saigon at first light on 10 December, at 5 a.m., heading towards the reported location of Force Z. They spread out into a huge fan as they flew south to the search area. Then, at 6.25 a.m., the first of 85 twin-engine Nell and Betty long-range bombers started to take off from Saigon; 34 carried bombs and 51 carried torpedoes. The Betty bombers carried extra fuel and would later earn the name from Americans who shot them down as 'Flying cigars' for the way they burnt and blew up when hit. There were so many bombers to organize that the last bombers only left the ground at 8 a.m.

Right: Mitsubishi G4M 'Betty' Bombers

Below: Force Z destroyer HMS Tenedos

The ten squadrons of Nells and Bettys flew in small formations of eight or nine aircraft, and climbed slowly up to 10,000 feet. The visibility was excellent, with only small patches of low cloud. The planes of six of the squadrons carried torpedoes, and the other four squadrons carried bombs. They flew slowly south at their most economical speed – it was up to the nine reconnaissance aircraft well ahead of them to the south to find the enemy and direct them in. However, hours passed without word of Force Z being located, and soon the bombers had passed the danger-line of 400 nautical miles for their fuel supplies. Still, there was no report of the British naval force, and the pilots started to become anxious about their fuel position.

At 9.43 a.m., one of the reconnaissance planes spotted the destroyer *Tenedos* near Tioman Island. The detached destroyer was well on her way back to Singapore. The discovery of the destroyer was reported back and at 10.15 a.m., three squadrons totalling 25 aircraft converged on *Tenedos*. The first flight of nine bombers dropped 500kg bombs at the sleek destroyer far below – but they all missed the fast and agile destroyer by several hundred feet. With their bombs gone, those bombers were now out of the fight and turned for home. *Tenedos* broadcast that she was under attack – the signal was received by Force Z and caused great alarm. It would appear, however, that the radio transmission was not picked up in Singapore only 120 miles away, as no fleet-defence Buffalo fighters were sent out to assist. They could have been overhead within a relatively short period of time. The slow Japanese bombers had no fighter support from Zeros and would have been easy prey for the RAF Brewster Buffalo fighters if they had been requested.

The remaining eight Japanese reconnaissance planes were now well spread out and reaching the southern legs of their own search areas. Individually, they started to turn back to run north towards home – each would follow a different route north to cover as much sea as possible.

At 10.15 a.m., one reconnaissance plane spotted Force Z in the distance and sent out three radio signals reporting the location, heading, and make up of the force. A directional signal was also broadcast so that other Japanese planes could follow. The attack on *Tenedos* was immediately broken off.

11 a.m. The initial high-altitude bomb attack on *Repulse*

At 11 a.m., the first eight Japanese Mitsubishi bombers came into view of Force Z – each plane carrying a single 250kg bomb. In line abreast, the eight bombers flew over *Repulse* at a height of 10,000 feet – presenting a fine target to the battlecruiser's anti-aircraft guns. All ships in the squadron went to: 'Action Stations. Repel Aircraft'. Gun-crews rushed to their stations and soon the Japanese planes were close enough for the control officers of the high-angle guns to start the plot of their range, height and speed.

The order to fire was given: 'Commence. Commence. Commence.' But no radio signal of any kind regarding the contact went out from the flagship to Singapore: radio silence was still being observed. Both ships hoisted the White Ensign – the traditional battle ensign – to their fore and main masts, and signal flags on *Prince of Wales* were run up directing the force to turn together 30 degrees to starboard. Here was a fast, modern flagship in the Royal Navy attempting a fleet manoeuvre of a squadron in unison by signal flag.

Four of the much vaunted 5.25-inch high-elevation turrets on the starboard side of *Prince of Wales* could now train on the enemy aircraft and these opened up first of all when the gunnery officers in fire control were getting good readings, at about 12,000 yards.

The World War I battlecruiser *Repulse* had a secondary armament of 12 rapid-fire 4-inch guns – but these guns were designed primarily to counter broadside attacks by fast moving surface vessels and were of no great use against aircraft. With only a scattering of anti-aircraft weaponry, comprising six old four-inch anti-aircraft guns, three 'Pom-Pom' guns, and some cannons and machine guns, she was not well equipped to counter a massed modern aircraft threat from the skies. The gunners on *Repulse,* at action stations and clad in their tin helmets and anti-flash hoods and gloves, opened up at about 11,000 yards with their high level anti-aircraft guns.

It was immediately noticed that the anti-aircraft shells from both ships were exploding to the right of the Japanese aircraft – who were not taking any evading action at all. The aircraft continued to fly a straight course towards *Repulse*. The swing of both ships to starboard signalled by the flagship was counteracting the corrections to the left being given to the guns. The turn to starboard soon caused all the guns on the starboard side of both ships to cease firing, as the huge superstructure of the ships started to mask their line of fire.

Phillips then signalled by flags that all ships were to turn together 50 degrees to port. But ships the size of capital ships took time to answer the helm, and although the helms were put over to port, the ships' momentum continued the initial swing to starboard – so much so that their port side guns came into action and started firing. But then the turn to port started to take effect and the port side guns, with their lines of fire now being masked by the superstructure, had to cease fire. For a few moments, no guns fired at all, before the turn to port allowed the starboard side guns to come back into action once again.

These cumbersome fleet manoeuvres by signal flag had robbed the gunnery officers of the opportunity to settle down to a long run of firing that would have enabled corrections to be

Repulse (at the bottom) is hit and straddled by Japanese bombs at the start of the engagement as Prince of Wales *(top right) manoeuvres at high speed. (IWM)*

steadily applied and more effective fire brought to bear at the unswerving compact formation of Japanese aircraft – which still came on at a steady speed and steady height. Perhaps realising that fleet manoeuvres were inappropriate, Phillips then gave orders to the commanders of the other ships that individual ships had freedom of manoeuvre.

At around 11.30 a.m., the first eight Nell bombers attacking *Repulse* released their bombs simultaneously. Most landed in the water within a radius of 10 metres of the battlecruiser. *Repulse* was straddled either side – with one tall column of water erupting skywards on the starboard side, followed by several more on the port side.

One small 250kg bomb successfully struck *Repulse* amidships, penetrating through the port seaplane hanger and bursting on the armoured deck below, causing a number of casualties. A Walrus seaplane was damaged and had to be pushed over the side into the sea. *Repulse* emerged from the spray with a small plume of smoke coming from her upper deck where she had been struck. Her speed was unaffected and she steamed on, trailing just the small curl of smoke. Five of the Japanese planes had been hit – two so seriously that they had to leave the battle with their one remaining bomb undropped and fly straight back to their airfield.

With the first bombing wave over, Force Z steamed on southwards towards Singapore. But within minutes, radar on *Prince of Wales* picked up an even larger force of aircraft approaching, not from the north as expected, but from the south-east. These planes had flown as far south as Singapore in their search for Force Z and were now running back north to press home an attack on Force Z.

11.38 a.m. Torpedo attack on *Prince of Wales*

At 11.38 a.m., 17 high-level bombers and 50 torpedo-bombers coming up from the south-east now joined the six remaining aircraft of the first wave. The Japanese aircraft manouevered into position for the next wave of attacks, circling the two capital ships.

The Japanese aircraft started their attack from about 8 miles away. Two squadrons separated whilst outwith the range of British guns and manouevered to be able to approach from different directions. They made simultaneous attacks on both capital ships in a pincer-like formation designed to split up British anti-aircraft gunfire.

The bombers flew up from the south-east and then crossed the bows of the British ships still well out of range. They then started forming up in line astern, as they increased their speed and began to drop towards the British squadron, bearing a little ahead of Force Z. The Japanese aircrew scanned the sky for signs of the RAF fighters that they expected to appear at any time: the battle was well within the RAF range from Singapore and Kuantan.

Phillips ordered Force Z to work up to 25 knots to present a more difficult target for the bombers – the captains of his ships had by now been given freedom to manoeuvre. On the bridge of *Prince of Wales*, an officer commented that the circling aircraft appeared to be carrying torpedoes. Phillips replied that there were no such aircraft about.

The Japanese aircraft continued to lose height and flew into some low cloud, before appearing off *Prince of Wales's* port bow. The first line of nine twin-engine bombers, each carrying torpedoes armed with 150kg warheads, started their initial attack run at a speed of 150 knots (about 180 mph) and at a height of about 35–55 metres. The line of nine aircraft then split up in three neat turns: three aircraft to each turn, to face *Prince of Wales*. The nine aircraft were now flying in a huge extended arc directly towards the port side of Admiral Phillips' flagship.

As the Japanese planes came into range, all eight port-side 5.25-inch guns opened fire. They were soon joined by the single Bofors gun on the quarterdeck, then the four sets of eight-barreled 'Pom-Poms' pumping out their 2-pounder shells, and finally by the Oerlikons and machine guns.

Tracers arced up towards the black dots in the sky, and after 12 salvoes, the 5.25-inch guns moved from controlled-fire at individual planes to barrage-fire, throwing up a curtain of bursting shells to provide a dangerous flak barrier for the hostile planes and try to force them to drop their torpedoes early. The British anti-aircraft gunners, however, were unprepared for the sheer speed of the Japanese bombers, which were flying in on their attack runs at the equivalent of 180mph. Royal Navy torpedo-bombers were old, much slower Swordfish biplanes that attacked at less than 100mph. Most of the British anti-aircraft shells burst well behind the aircraft as they flashed down towards the British ships.

As the Japanese planes swooped in at 180mph, their torpedoes were released when they were between 1,500 metres and 600 metres from *Prince of Wales*. One torpedo exploded as it hit the water. Captain Leach gave the order: 'Hard a-port'; to attempt to comb the tracks of the torpedoes, and this turn forced one plane to lose its aim – it banked away and headed instead for *Repulse*. The torpedoes had been set to run at a depth of 6 metres at 25 knots.

British naval 'Pom-Pom' anti-aircraft gun – the Chicago Piano

The Japanese bombers were too large and too fast for them to pull away quickly after they had dropped their torpedoes. After dropping them, the bombers flew straight at *Prince of Wales* machine-gunning as they came – reaching the battleship well before their torpedoes did.

One of the eight aircraft was shot down on its attack run, but two torpedoes successfully struck the ship's hull. A column of water was seen to erupt on the port side of *Prince of Wales* – the outer hull was holed, but only limited flooding of the compartment between the outer hull and the inner hull was caused.

At about 11.44 a.m., however, a second torpedo struck what is a battleship's Achilles heel: the unarmoured area at the stern outwith the armoured box of the 'citadel'.

The vital elements of a battleship: its engines, magazines, the armoured cylinders called 'barbettes' that run up from the magazines at the bottom of the ship to the gun turrets themselves, are all protected inside the citadel. The armoured box of the citadel in the case of *Prince of Wales* was made up of made up of a vertical main armour belt 14.7 inches thick, running along both sides of the hull from in front of the forward gun turrets to aft of the stern turrets. The armour belt tapered to 5.5 inches thick at its ends. Armoured bulkheads 11.7 inches thick forward, and 9.8 inches and 4 inches aft ran across the ship athwartships, forward of the foremost main gun turret, and aft of the aftmost gun turret.

The citadel was protected from plunging fire by a horizontal armour deck up to 6 inches thick on the main deck (above the magazines) with a lower deck horizontal armoured deck up to 5 inches thick and tapering to 2.5 inches at the front and 4 inches at the stern. The citadel was almost indestructible and made a battleship almost unsinkable – but not quite.

It is not possible to protect by armour the vital parts that make a ship move and push the ship through the water – such as the rudder, the propellers and the brackets that hold and support the free section of propeller shaft (which comes out from the hull to the propeller itself). These need to be in free water to operate. *Prince of Wales* had four propellers, two to either side of the hull. Each of the four was driven from its own engine room located 200–250 feet forward from the stern.

The torpedo from this wave of the air attack struck *Prince of Wales* under her stern, beside the outer port propeller shaft, blasting open a hole in her hull some 4 metres high and 6 metres wide. This torpedo strike in such a vulnerable area dealt a critical blow, which set in motion a chain of events that would lead directly to the loss of the great ship.

The torpedo detonated on the hull bottom, just forward of the bracket that supported the free section of the outer port propeller shaft. The explosion was just aft of, and very close to, the stern tube from which the free outboard shaft emerged from the hull to the propeller. The explosion on the hull was right beside the tube – and the shaft led 200–250 feet through the ship, all the way to B engine room. The tube and the free section of shaft were damaged, and water started to pour into her hull through the 4 metres high by 6 metres wide hole.

The propeller, driven by B engine room deep in the ship, continued to rotate at a high speed of some 204 revolutions per minute. However, now damaged, it was turning out of centre, and this caused it to start to vibrate violently. This caused further weakening of the shaft support struts holding the free section of shaft in place. All along its path, 200–250 feet along inside the ship to B engine room, the vibrating shaft started to cause internal damage. The watertight glands around the shaft in several transverse bulkheads (frames) along its

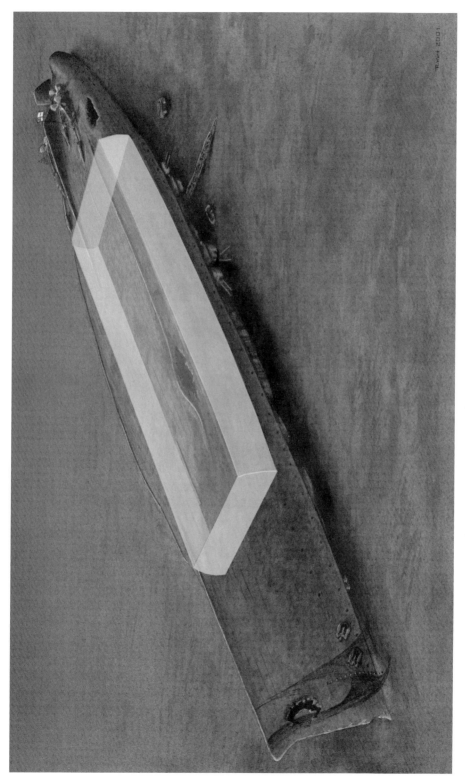

The wreck of the Prince of Wales with the citadel area highlighted

route were compromised and the immediate bulkhead surrounding the shaft damaged. This created a direct route for water to flood up the prop shaft alley and get into B engine room and its associated action machinery room and diesel dynamo room. When an attempt was made to restart the turbine, before the extent of the damage was known, this resulted in the complete destruction of the previously damaged shaft tunnel bulkheads. There was now a direct route for water into the very heart of the ship.

The *Prince of Wales* had been making 24 knots before the torpedo struck. With the shutting down of one of her four engines and the loss of drive from one of her four massive propellers, her speed immediately started to drop. As water flooded into her hull through the large hole and searched up the shaft alley, it was soon rising fast in the B engine room bilges. Emergency pumps were started but they were unable to stop the steady rise of the water – it soon became clear that B engine room itself would have to be evacuated. The vital turbines would be left in operation but the machinery would be prepared to run underwater. Once the water was over the platform where the controls were situated, B engine room was evacuated. As the last man got out and the hatch was being dogged down, water started oozing out.

Near to B engine room was Y engine room, which drove the inner port propeller shaft, situated close to the damaged outer port propeller shaft. As crew strove to deal with the problems in B engine room, loud crashing sounds were heard in Y engine room – forcing this engine also to be shut down.

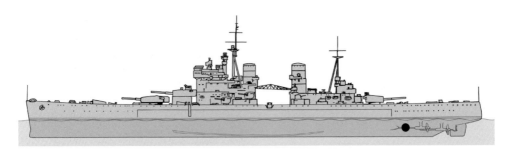

Location of the critical port-side torpedo strike on Prince of Wales

Prince of Wales *listed to port and settled down by the stern after the port-side torpedo strike*

The damage to the outer port stern tube, to the shaft's internal supports and bulkhead glands had caused the shaft to rotate with difficulty and to vibrate violently. This, in turn, caused failure of bolting flanges along the length of the shaft. Eventually, the 17.5-inch thick shaft itself broke, and the shaft strut and propeller, along with a section of shaft aft of the last flange joint, broke away from the ship and fell to the seabed, ripping the stern tube out of the hull as it went. Some of these pieces of machinery and debris entered the inner port propeller race, damaging its blades and operation. This is believed to have been what caused the crashing sounds reported in Y engine room.

By 12.02 p.m., both port propellers were out of action. With only the two starboard shafts and propellers now working to push her through the water, *Prince of Wales*'s speed dropped to 15 knots.

As water flooded rapidly deep into her hull through the gaping hole, and started to run through the ship via the damage caused to her internal bulkheads, she began to list to port. She quickly took on a list of 11.5 degrees and settled down by the stern by 1.5 metres. The men on the bridge of one of the newest and most efficient fighting ships in the world could see another formation of torpedo-bombers preparing to attack *Repulse*. There were still 34 torpedo-bombers and 23 high-level bombers waiting to attack.

Torpedo attack on *Repulse*

It was now *Repulse*'s turn to meet the torpedo-bombers, as some 15 Mitsubishis started their attack runs. *Repulse* was not well equipped to deal with an aircraft attack. She had twenty 4-inch guns, but some of these guns could not elevate to a high enough level and others could not depress sufficiently to engage low-flying aircraft. Their control systems were old-fashioned, and many were not power-operated and had to be trained by hand. Her guns scored little success against the Japanese aircraft, but she had survived relatively unscathed so far.

At 11.58 a.m., Captain Tennant aboard *Repulse*, seeing the flagship *Prince of Wales* starting to list, broke radio silence and radioed Singapore for help. This was the first information HQ at Singapore had received about Force Z's exact location since the signal Phillips had ordered *Tenedos* to broadcast earlier that morning at 8 a.m., advising that the British ships were returning to Singapore and asking for destroyer support on 11 December near the Anambas Islands. It was the first knowledge HQ had of the diversion to Kuantan, or that Japanese aircraft were attacking. Some have suggested that if when the first Japanese reconnaissance aircraft were sighted, Singapore had been advised, RAF fighters could perhaps have arrived above Force Z before the first attack. The Japanese long-range bombers had no fighter escort and they would have made easy prey for even the much-criticised Buffalo fighters. But in the event, all four RAF Brewster Buffalo Fighter squadrons were still on the ground at Singapore. Eleven Brewster Buffalo fighters were ordered to take off once Captain Tennant's radio signal was received – but by then it was too late. The scene of the battle was one hour's flying time away. As the attacks were going in on the two capital ships, the three escort destroyers brought every gun they had to bear on the Japanese aircraft, whilst simultaneously searching for any submarine contacts on ASDIC.

As the Japanese aircraft dived at *Repulse* on their attack runs, Captain Tennant turned his great ship swiftly towards the diving aircraft – as he positioned his ship to comb the tracks of the torpedoes that he knew would soon be released. The torpedoes were dropped, and as they ran in the water they left tell tale trails of white bubbles. Captain Tennant showed great skill as he managed to comb the tracks of every one of the torpedoes dropped by the two Japanese squadrons, as well as the overs from the attack on *Prince of Wales*. The crew spoke later with pride of 19 torpedoes being combed and how the huge ship had been thrown about like a destroyer. He also successfully avoided all the bombs from high-level bombers dropped from 12,000 feet – timed to coincide exactly with the torpedo-bombers making their attack.

12 noon. The lull

The torpedo-bombers from this wave of the attack turned away about 12 noon, pursued by the last rounds of *Repulse's* anti-aircraft fire. As her guns ceased, something of a lull descended on the battle scene and this allowed crews on both ships to assess the damage so far. *Prince of Wales* was wallowing along at her reduced speed of 15 knots. *Repulse* was some 3 miles away from her flagship, relatively undamaged and in fine fighting form. An uncanny, ominous silence descended on what had been a frenetic scene, just minutes before. The sea was a beautiful, silky calm.

Following the aft torpedo strike on *Prince of Wales* – and its immediate consequences – massive damage had been sustained to the electrical system at the stern. The after 5.25-inch dual-purpose turrets (anti-aircraft or surface targets) had lost electrical power and been put out of action – as had the ship's radars and her vital steering gear. Without power, both the steering motors were dead – the steering gear jammed, and with the rudder not functioning and only her starboard propellers pushing her, the great ship began to veer in a slow turn to port.

Internal communications were also seriously effected, and this made it difficult for the efforts of damage-control teams to be directed effectively. The teams did manage to rig emergency electrical leads to vital functions and establish a flooding boundary, whilst attempting to restore the steering.

To try and counter the list to port and stern down attitude of the ship, Captain Leach ordered the flooding of the forward void spaces of the starboard torpedo-defence system. He needed the ship level, or almost level, so that its AA guns could be trained. But flooding the outer and inner voids of the defence system with incompressible water made the ship more vulnerable, should she be struck there by torpedo. By 12.10 p.m., the counter-flooding had managed to reduce the list to port by about 2.5 degrees to 9 degrees. The 'out of control' signal flag was hoisted.

The substantial flooding of the various rooms in the immediate vicinity of the torpedo strike, as well as B engine room, the action machinery room and the diesel dynamo room, accelerated and expanded upwards and inboard through the ship. In the heat of the moment, some personnel left watertight hatches open or insufficiently dogged down. There was significant flooding on the middle deck forward of the main aftmost (Y) gun turret and barbette.

Although the after 5.25-inch dual-purpose guns had been put out of action by the power loss, the list to port also adversely affected the remaining operational forward anti-aircraft guns. Internal communications and systems for the training and elevation of both the 5.25-inch weapons and the 'Pom-Poms' were thrown into disarray. With the 11.5-degree list at that time, not one of the eight power-operated 5.25-inch gun turrets could be trained properly. The situation was becoming increasingly desperate, as the massed Japanese bombers manouevered for another attacking run in the skies overhead.

With the loss or reduction of electric power in the aft section of the ship, many of the rooms, corridors and companionways were plunged into darkness. Electric fans stopped working and the temperature inside these sections of the ship began to soar. Dim emergency lighting did come on in the stern section, but that also failed, as emergency power from the dynamos housed in the flooded dynamo room was lost.

Gunnery officers took advantage of the lull to visit their gun positions, to call for specialist ordnance or electrical ratings to repair damage. Casualties were tended to and heaps of spent cartridges from the guns cleared and dumped over the side. Where ammunition power-hoists had failed, men formed chains to pass up cases of ammunition for the smaller guns or heavy shells for the larger guns, from the magazines deep in the bowels of the ship. During the lull, *Electra* and *Vampire* were ordered to search in the wake of *Prince of Wales* for men believed to have been blown overboard by the shock of the torpedo explosion – nobody was found.

12.19 p.m. The final round

Starboard torpedo attack on *Prince of Wales*

At 12.19 p.m., as the crew of *Prince of Wales* fought to restore control and redress the list, the final round of the battle began. Crew on the beleaguered ships spotted a large formation of aircraft to the east losing height and splitting into two attack formations. With her rudder still jammed, *Prince of Wales* was unable to manoeuvre. As the great ship listed to port, so her starboard side rolled higher out of the water. Her anti-aircraft guns on that side would not be able to depress sufficiently to hit the oncoming aircraft as they made their low flying torpedo attack runs just 100 feet or so above the water. With the operation of the 5.25-inch dual-purpose secondary armament and the 'Pom-Pom' anti-aircraft guns and radars all compromised by the list and power failure, *Prince of Wales* had been left with little anti-aircraft protection. The few guns aboard that could still fire opened up.

At 12.20 p.m., *Prince of Wales* finally broke radio silence and transmitted a signal, advising that she had been struck by a torpedo on the port side, that *Repulse* also had been struck, and requested that destroyers be sent. No request was made for aircraft support.

The catastrophe wrought on one of Britain's finest and newest battleships by just the one torpedo strike must have seemed unbelievable to those aboard. Battleships had been considered virtually unsinkable – and yet, in just under half an hour, Churchill's favourite battleship had been turned into an un-steerable, sinking, indefensible, water-filled hulk.

Nine minutes earlier, at 12.10 p.m., when *Prince of Wales* had hoisted the 'out of control' signal flag, Captain Tennant on *Repulse* decided to close on *Prince of Wales* to see if assistance could be given. When *Repulse* had closed to just over 800 yards from *Prince of Wales*, 26 more Japanese planes massed for a torpedo attack on the two capital ships. Initially, these planes appeared to close on the crippled *Prince of Wales* (now moving at only 10–15 knots) from the starboard bow, but as *Repulse* closed her, three of these bombers veered off to attack *Repulse*.

Six bombers came in low and attacked *Prince of Wales* on her raised starboard side, able to fly under the anti-aircraft fire she could offer on that side. Three torpedoes from this attack struck in quick succession. These torpedoes were armed with a larger 205kg warhead than the 150kg torpedo that struck her port side in the first wave of the attack.

One of the three torpedoes stuck the hull a few metres back from the bow itself and forward of the citadel bulkhead – almost directly beneath the forward of the two starboard anchors. A jagged hole some seven metres in diameter tore right through the ship as the torpedo blast blew clean out through the port side. This damage caused the immediate flooding of the two peak tanks and possibly the aviation fuel tanks behind them in addition, although there was no fire.

A second torpedo struck at the very bottom of the main vertical armour belt in the forward section of the ship, almost directly under B turret, and a plume of oil and water shot up the side of the ship. The torpedo struck the unarmoured section of the hull (beneath the armour belt) where there was only the 1-inch-thick steel of the ship's hull bottom.

The blast from this torpedo opened a hole some 7 metres in diameter directly into the inner lower sections of the ship. The side-protection system inner voids in this area had earlier been flooded in an attempt to counter the port list, and the outer voids had also been flooded when it became clear that the first phase of counter-flooding had not been effective. As part of the counter-flooding, washrooms on the lower deck and living spaces on the middle deck had all been flooded with salt water and oil.

But essential though the flooding had been, incompressible water in these rooms and voids prevented them from functioning as designed in the side-protection system, and allowed much of the energy from the torpedo explosion to be vented into the ship itself. Had the starboard side not been raised by the port list, this torpedo would have struck the main armour belt, which would have taken the impact with little damage. With the blast having struck at the very bottom edge of the armour belt, even if the list had been just a few feet less, the armour belt would have taken the hit without difficulty.

The third torpedo struck the starboard side of the hull just aft of Y turret, leaving a hole 11 metres long and 4 metres high, and jamming the outer starboard side propeller shaft. This brought the turbines for one of the two remaining still-functioning engine rooms to an abrupt halt. Only the inner starboard-side propeller was now working – and the speed of the great ship was now reduced to 8 knots.

These three torpedo hits instantly negated all the damage-control efforts to contain the flooding at the stern. As water flooded into the starboard-side spaces, the port list was reduced from 9 degrees to 3 degrees. As the ship took on more water, however, she settled deeper into the water – and this lead to uncontrollable progressive flooding.

Location of the three torpedo strikes on the starboard side of Prince of Wales. *The aftmost strike is higher up the side of the ship, due to her stern settling after the first port torpedo strike*

Repulse attacked from all directions

The remaining twenty or so torpedo-bombers almost simultaneously attacked *Repulse* from different directions. The first eight aircraft dropped their torpedoes on her starboard side. Captain Tennant turned *Repulse* to starboard to comb the tracks again – but then the three aircraft, which had peeled off from the attack on the starboard side of *Prince of Wales* attacked *Repulse* on her port side. *Repulse* was in an impossible situation and could not avoid both salvoes of torpedoes. Captain Tennant could do no more than continue his turn to starboard to avoid the first eight torpedoes.

One torpedo hit *Repulse* amidships on the port side, holing the outer hull, but doing little significant damage. The ship was well protected here by her torpedo bulge and she took the hit well, continuing to manoeuvre and steam at 25 knots – but another torpedo hit and jammed her rudder. She took on a list but counter flooding steps started immediately on the other side of the ship.

Immediately afterwards, the nine aircraft of the third Kanoya squadron, which had been intending to attack *Prince of Wales*, swooped down to attack *Repulse*, with orders to split up and attack *Repulse* from different angles. Six aircraft attempted to work their way round to her starboard side, whilst the remaining three Betty bombers went straight in at her port side. It was a skillfully executed attack. *Repulse*'s engines were still fully functioning but with her rudder jammed she was reduced to steaming in a wide circle.

The three Betty bombers attacking the port side approached to about 500 metres before releasing their torpedoes. Another two, possibly three, hits were scored. After releasing their torpedoes, the Japanese aircraft overflew *Repulse*, machine-gunning her decks and scattering British sailors as they ran for cover. Two of the three Japanese aircraft were hit by 'Pom-Pom' shells and crashed into the sea, one in a ball of fire. Water poured into the ship through the holes in her hull from these hits and she started to list to port.

At 12.25 p.m., the other six torpedo-bombers attacking *Repulse*'s starboard side scored another single hit. In the course of four to five minutes, *Repulse* had been hit by four, possibly five, torpedoes. Very quickly the list to port started to increase.

At 12.30 p.m., this last series of devastating attacks on *Repulse* died away.

All 51 of the Japanese torpedo-bombers had now completed their attacks, but only eight of the 34 high-level bombers had done so. There remained two squadrons of high-level bombers that had not yet attacked and each plane carried a single 500kg bomb. At 12.33 p.m., the first nine of these bombers started a high-altitude attack, but their bombs were dropped early and all failed to find their target, missing by some considerable distance.

12.32 p.m. *Repulse* sinks

Repulse, with multiple large holes in her hull, was now sinking quickly. The two destroyers *Electra* and *Vampire* stood by her.

Once it was clear the ship was lost, Captain Tennant ordered all hands to the main deck, the Carley floats to be cut loose and the ship abandoned. Throughout the ship, officers or senior ratings fell their men out and ordered them to get up on deck. Not one single man of the experienced mainly pre-war crew is recorded as having left his place of duty until ordered to do so.

Dozens of men now came pouring up through hatches from below or scrambled down ladders from stations high in the superstructure. Where possible, Carley floats – life rafts made of copper with watertight subdivisions and covered in cork and canvas – were released from their fixings.

The crew started jumping over the side into a spreading pool of oil. As the ship progressively and quickly listed further, men had to climb up the sloping deck to get away from the superstructure and top hamper that was now starting to loom over them. They climbed over the guardrails and then slid down the huge raised starboard side of the battlecruiser. As she rolled further over to port, the huge torpedo bulge and its jagged torpedo hole raised out of the water. Men slid down the side of the ship until they reached the top of the bulge before going over it and into the water. Hundreds of men got away in the course of a few minutes – it was quite orderly with no panic and pushing. The men queued and waited for their turn to go down the side.

One officer mistimed his jump into the water and fell back into the ship through the torpedo hole in her side. A group of marines jumped off the stern into the still-turning propeller blades. Captain Tennant himself was swept off the tilting deck as she rolled to port and surfaced alongside a raft.

Where loud-speakers below decks had broken down, some men in compartments only realised too late that the order to abandon ship had been given, and had to force open dogged down hatches above them, often against the list of the ship, to fight their way up to deck. The cries of other men now trapped inside the hull could be heard coming up ventilation shafts.

The progressive heel over to port was interrupted as *Repulse* gave a sudden lurch. She rolled over on her beam ends, exactly on her side, with masts, funnel and superstructure at water level. She seemed to pause there on her side momentarily and men walked across her now seemingly horizontal starboard side to jump in the water. The inexorable roll of the ship then continued on again as the great weight of her gun turrets and superstructure pulled her over. She rolled further over and the stern reared up to expose her still turning propellers. The stern then sunk and disappeared, leaving her bow hanging in the air. Given the depth of water – just short of 60 metres – and the length of the great ship, the stern may have impacted the seabed as the bows stuck up from the water. There is no doubt that some crew trapped inside were still alive at this point, fighting for survival as the ship rolled completely over. Just 11 minutes after the first torpedo had struck her, her majestic flared bows disappeared beneath the water. It is a disconcerting thought that as the ship settled on the bottom there may still have been crew trapped in air pockets at their stations in sealed-off compartments, waiting for the end as water slowly crept in through pipework and ducting.

By 12.32 p.m., *Repulse* was gone. A few bloops of air and fuel escaped the sunken ship and broke the surface amid floating bodies, debris and a slick of black oil. Men struggled in the water to swim away from the oil with their life-jackets on. Once clear, some started singing, whilst others cracked jokes to keep spirits up. There was much fear of sharks and moments of panic as swimmers thought something had brushed their legs under the water. Some men deliberately swam into the patches of oil to avoid possible shark attacks. Some dead sharks floated on the water, but no doubt any live sharks had been scared well away from the battle scene. Men who could swim struck out for the Carley floats and these soon became little oases of oil-soaked, blackened, wounded men. A formation of Japanese aircraft was spotted coming overhead and many men jumped off the Carley floats fearing they were about to be machine-gunned. The Japanese Mitsubishi aircraft flew over their heads without opening fire on the highly-trained and valuable crew struggling in the water below. There is a report that one *Repulse* survivor saw a Japanese pilot saluting where *Repulse* had gone down.

12.41 p.m. Final bombing attack on *Prince of Wales*

At 12.41 p.m., lookouts on the stricken *Prince of Wales* reported eight high-level Nell bombers approaching in a tight formation from ahead, seemingly wing tip to wing tip. What was believed to be the periscope of a submarine was also reported.

Prince of Wales opened fire with every gun that was still functioning. Three of the forward 5.25-inch high-elevation guns fired well, but the fourth had to cease fire due to an oil leak in the turret hydraulic gear. Despite her dire predicament, shells from those forward 5.25-inch gun turrets were still able to damage five of these aircraft, despite S1 and S2 being hampered in their firing due to their range-taker having been wounded in the right eye, forcing an estimated height to be used.

Once in position, the Japanese planes dropped seven 500kg bombs from 2,560 metres (the release mechanism failed on the eighth plane). The crew of the battleship watched as the bombs started their casual fall towards the stricken ship and sought cover where they could. A hand-klaxon sounded on the bridge, as Admiral Phillips ordered everyone to the deck.

Two bombs exploded in the water either side of the great ship and one bomb struck her, penetrating the catapult deck on her port side and exploding on the 5-inch-thick armoured deck in the cinema flat. Here, 200–300 men were being treated in an emergency first aid station, and there were heavy casualties. Fragments and shards of metal riddled the ship's sides and air intakes, allowing additional flooding amidships. Side-scuttles were distorted and this allowed water to flow into the middle deck. The fumes and blast from the bomb's explosion and its flash also forced a way through shafts into X boiler room, situated a little away beneath the armoured deck, and caused casualties amongst the personnel there. The explosion caused the steam flow from X boiler room to X engine room (driving the one remaining working propeller) to be lost.

1.18 p.m. 'H.M.S. *PRINCE OF WALES* SUNK'

With all her propellers now out of action, with no power or steering capability, *Prince of Wales* slewed to a stop in the smooth seas. As the bombers broke off their attack, an uncanny silence descended on the great ship; the guns ceased firing and the engines were stopped.

The huge battleship was steadily settling deeper by the stern into the water. Survivors commented that it looked 'as though the tide was coming in'. By 12.50 p.m., the end was near – she had taken on an estimated 18,000 tons of water.

Prince of Wales sent out another signal, asking for all available tugs to be sent to her assistance. Then another confused signal was sent, which was not understood at Singapore. There was no mention that *Repulse* had sunk 20 minutes earlier. Captain Leach ordered that the wounded be got away in Carley floats and other wounded were sent across on stretchers to the destroyer *Express*, which had come alongside to render assistance. Whereas the old battlecruiser *Repulse* had gone down within 11 minutes of the first torpedo hit, *Prince of Wales* had been crippled 50 minutes before *Repulse* sank and had lingered for a further 50 minutes after she went. Her crew had more time to prepare themselves for the passing of their ship. Carley floats had been filled with wounded men and then floated off gently from the stern as she went slowly under, shortly after the last bombing attack.

Captain Leach left the bridge and came down to the quarterdeck, where a large group of crew had congregated. He calmly told them that the ship was still a fighting unit and asked for volunteers to stay and try to assist in getting the ship back to Singapore. There were some volunteers and Captain Leach gave permission for those men not needed to man the guns or other vital services to get across to *Express*. He then climbed back up to the bridge to join Admiral Phillips. Hundreds of men started crossing over to *Express* on makeshift lines and gangplanks. But as *Prince of Wales* rolled further over onto her port side and her starboard side lifted up, the gap between her starboard side and *Express* started to widen. The gangplanks fell into the sea, but men continued to swing across on ropes and the cable that still joined the two ships. Others tried to jump the gap – some succeeded, but others failed and fell down in between the ships. The cable finally snapped under the strain.

At 1 p.m., X engine room personnel were ordered to secure the turbines and by 1.15 p.m. – an hour and a half after the first torpedo hit – the list to port started to appreciably worsen. It was clear the ship was now well beyond any help from aircraft, destroyers, or tugs. The order was given: 'Abandon Ship'. She would remain afloat for just eight more minutes.

As the battleship's starboard bilge keel rose up, the skipper of *Express* skillfully judged the last moment before he was forced to pull away, her hull bumping and grinding on the battleship's heaving keel and almost being overturned. The destroyer suffered a 20-ft gash in her hull from the contact – but many men had been saved. As she pulled away, men were left on *Prince of Wales* queuing at the rails and forced to slide or leap into the oil-covered water. The hull of *Prince of Wales* had so nearly capsized *Express* as it rose up under her, that several crew and survivors were tipped into the sea, or jumped in, thinking the destroyer was in fact capsizing.

There were several hundred men left on the battleship and they now congregated at the highest points of the ship, the fo'c'stle, and starboard-side quarterdeck – some almost casually standing and chatting or smoking. The gun crews on the upper decks still remained at their stations.

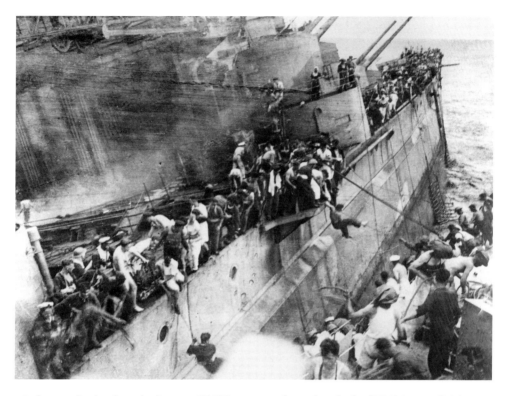

A photograph taken from the destroyer HMS Express, *on the starboard side of HMS* Prince of Wales, *as crew crowd the decks and scramble across ropes from the sinking battleship. (IWM)*

A large-scale evacuation over the starboard side now started – men walking or sliding down the great starboard side of the battleship to jump into the water 40 feet below. A forest of bobbing heads and bodies were swimming hard to get away from the ship lest they be carried down by the suction. Now that her end was imminent, the gun crews were released from their duties, officers counting their men to make sure all were present before ordering them to blow up their life jackets and get over the side.

Prince of Wales heeled right over onto her port side – but not as quickly as *Repulse* had done. Several dozen men walked calmly down the starboard side of the great ship as it hung almost upside down on the surface for a few minutes. Then, her great sleek bow slowly rose in the air.

Hundreds of men struggling in the water or safe on *Express* watched the great ship's passing. Her bows reared high in the air, the large torpedo hole in her forepeak clearly visible. There was a great commotion and noise from inside the ship as fixtures tore loose inside her and fell downwards. She then disappeared by the stern. Some sailors saluted as she went under; some cried. The whole action had taken 100 minutes.

Admiral Sir Tom Phillips had remained on the bridge almost to the end – he and Captain Leach were seen to be silent and impervious to entreaties to abandon ship before it was too late. There are reports of them being seen on the horizontal side of the battleship at about 1.24 p.m., as she rolled to port and capsized. Admiral Phillips' body and that of Captain Leach were later found floating in the water. As she went under, there were still several men standing on her hull, waiting for the end very calmly; some sat on her bottom and handed round cigarettes. Many were pulled under by the suction as the great ship finally went down, but several bobbed back up to the surface thanks to their lifebelts. The destroyer *Electra* sent a simple signal to GHQ in Singapore at 1.18 p.m.: 'H.M.S. *PRINCE OF WALES* SUNK'. It was one of nine signals sent during the action – none of which had requested RAF assistance.

With the slower rate of sinking of *Prince of Wales* compared to *Repulse*, and the assistance rendered by *Express* in taking so many men off, four out of every five crew on *Prince of Wales* were saved.

1.20 p.m. RAF aircraft arrive on scene

The first RAF aircraft – a pair of Brewster Buffalo fighters – arrived on the scene just three minutes before the *Prince of Wales* turned turtle. The badly listing battleship was seen drifting in a great slick of oil. Her anti-aircraft guns opened up on the RAF planes, mistaking them for more Japanese aircraft – but the RAF crew fired a flare from a Very pistol to give the recognition signal.

Shortly afterwards, ten more RAF Buffalo fighters arrived on scene, just in time to see *Prince of Wales* sink on the horizon. Japanese aircraft were still watching the scene unfold beneath them, but as the Buffalo fighters were sighted, the vulnerable Japanese bombers made off at high speed (even though the Buffaloes were slightly faster) and disappeared into cloud. By the time the flight of Buffaloes were above the site of the battle, there was not a single Japanese aircraft to be seen – just hundreds of men clinging to wreckage or life rafts in the midst of a vast, oil slick. The belated arrival of the air-cover Force Z had so badly needed brought jeers and booing from the men in the water. A Walrus seaplane returned directly to Singapore, landing at Seletar. The pilot and observer went straight to the operations room with grim faces, to report that *Prince of Wales* and *Repulse* had both been sunk.

Thankfully, the weather that day was fine – the seas were calm and warm. With several hours of daylight left, conditions were ideal for the location and rescue of survivors. Over the course of the next three hours, destroyers plucked 2,081 officers and men out of the sea. *Electra* and *Vampire* worked at the scene of *Repulse's* sinking, and *Express* at that of *Prince of Wales*, 8 miles away, where most were safely on Carley floats and boats launched during the more leisurely sinking. Scramble nets and lines were draped over the side of the destroyers and men struggled to reach the bottom of the nets and lines. Some did and were saved; others made it to the bottom of the nets and at the limit of their strength, fell back and disappeared. The most badly wounded were taken below for treatment, retching and coughing the oil out of their lungs. Rum was found to be an excellent remedy for swallowed oil, bringing on violent vomiting and a prompt recovery.

As survivors recovered, they started to rub the oil off themselves and wander round asking for missing pals and looking for a drink or a cigarette. Survivors tended to gravitate to familiar positions to offer help – gunners from *Repulse* taking over at the *Electra* guns, to allow the gun crew to be released for recovery work. Badly-scarred and flash-burned men started to suffer delayed shock. Morphine was administered, but soon there was a growing row of blanket-covered bodies.

The last man picked out of the water was a lone swimmer (thought initially only to be a drifting coconut) spotted from *Electra* swimming well in the distance. The navy ships left the scene finally at 4 p.m.

The grim toll in human lives in the final accounting was 840 men: 513 from *Repulse*; and 327 from *Prince of Wales*. The Japanese lost 18 dead in the three aircraft shot down.

The destroyers brought the survivors back to Singapore with the Brewster Buffalo fighters flying overhead as escort. The destroyer *Stronghold* and four US Navy destroyers steamed north from Singapore to conduct a further search of the battle area for survivors, but no more survivors were found.

Aftermath

The Japanese quickly broadcast news of the loss of the two capital ships – the attack had been a huge success for them. Knowing that there was no way such a great loss could be covered up, the sinkings were also acknowledged the British. Official word was immediately sent to London, where Churchill was told (taking time-difference into account) early on the morning of 10 December, whilst still in bed. He was stunned and later wrote that in all of the war he had never received a more direct shock. It had, after all, been Churchill who had insisted that *Prince of Wales* and *Repulse* go out to the Far East.

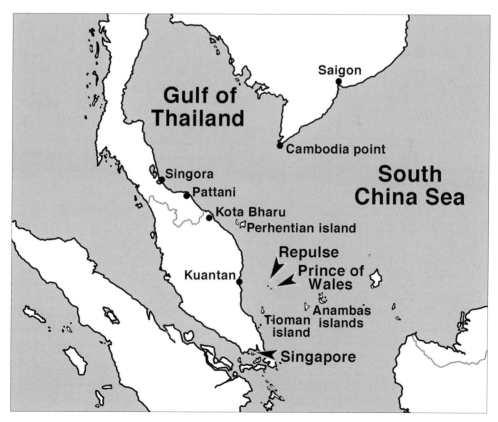

Chart of Malaya and the Gulf of Thailand showing location of the wrecks of HMS Prince of Wales *and* HMS Repulse

Churchill went forthwith to the House of Commons, and at 11.32 a.m., rose and made a statement to the House about the sinking – even as the destroyers of Force Z, crammed with survivors, were still on their way to Singapore.

Although the Admiralty reacted to the sinking by revisiting the plan to create a Far East Fleet in the Indian Ocean, by April 1942, not a single ship had been despatched to aid the defence of Singapore or the Malay Barrier.

Amongst Malaya's military and civilian population alike, there was stunned disbelief at the loss of two such great ships so soon after their arrival – and so soon after the outbreak of war with Japan. A sense of dread and foreboding now filled the hearts and minds of all those who feared a Japanese victory in Malaya. With *Repulse* and *Prince of Wales* now at the bottom of the South China Sea, the way was clear for the advancing Japanese force.

The Imperial Japanese Navy ruled supreme at sea.

FOOTNOTE: All four destroyers of Force Z survived the battle. HMS *Electra* was subsequently sunk just over two months later, in the Java Sea, on 27 February 1942, when her squadron was attacked by a large force of Japanese destroyers. HMS *Tenedos* was sunk by Japanese aircraft shortly afterwards, on 5 April 1942, off Colombo. Japanese dive-bombers sunk HMAS *Vampire* four days later, on 9 April 1942, off Ceylon.

Of the whole of Force Z, only HMS *Express*, who had boarded the crew from *Prince of Wales* as she sank, survived the war. Her hull was subsequently broken up at Vancouver in 1956.

CHAPTER NINE

THE FALL OF SINGAPORE

Now supreme in the Pacific, both at sea and in the air, Japanese forces swept across South-East Asia. Almost at a single stroke in the course of just 24 hours, the island fortress of Singapore had been denuded of two major elements for its defence: the RAF presence in Malaya had been crushed, and with the destruction of Force Z, the Royal Navy had been banished from the South China Sea. Even if the Singapore garrison could withstand a lengthy siege before a relief-force arrived, the island, once relieved, would still lie isolated, hundreds of miles behind enemy lines.

There was, in any event, no realistic likelihood of a naval relief-force being sent to bolster Singapore. The Royal Navy was already stretched to the limit by the war in Europe, which required that it keep its capital ships in the Atlantic and Mediterranean to defend Britain itself. The garrison of Malaya could have been stronger in numbers of troops and their quality, but to place such a radically larger force in such an exposed location would have been a significant risk. In the context of the situation in 1941–42, Singapore was strategically indefensible, and Churchill and his advisers did not make defence of the island a high priority.

Propaganda leaflets dropped from Japanese aircraft over-flying Singapore in January 1942 in the immediate run up to the Fall of Singapore. Author's collection

Terrible Riot In Singapore!
Secret Evacuated Of British Troops!

A terrible riot has broken out in Singapore!!
British and Australian Soldiers are being secretly evacuated from Singapore!.
Malayan and Indian Soldiers!. Pack up your troubles in your old kit bag and co-operate with the Nippon Army.
British and Australian Soldiers! Return to your homes at once by look or by crook. You may never get another chance to see your beloved ones in England and Australia!

Having landed their forces in Thailand and the northern Malayan Peninsula, Japanese troops now started to fight their way south towards Singapore. The British General Officer Commanding (Malaya) in Singapore, Lt. General Arthur Percival, believed that it was his duty to impose the maximum delay at every stage of the Japanese's southwards progress. He hoped to gain time for the arrival and deployment of reinforcements from Britain and her Empire. His strategy, however, had been fundamentally weakened and compromised by the disastrous RAF losses and the destruction of Force Z at sea.

Nevertheless, following his strategy of attempting to delay the Japanese advance, he refused to withdraw and relieve III Corps formations fighting in the north, which were on the point of collapse. This policy led to the 11th Indian Division being almost destroyed at Slim River, in a month-long engagement in northern and central Malaya. Other important battles were lost at Jitra and Layang Layang.

The Japanese continued their advance south, fighting towards Singapore. As they reached the Johor region at the very southern tip of the Malayan Peninsula, adjacent to Singapore Island, the time had come for the campaign's decisive battle to be fought, but the defending British and Empire forces were already dangerously weak. The British Army 18th Division had been sent to reinforce Singapore, but the main body of the relief-force was still en route and had yet to arrive. As a result, there was only a limited opportunity to build a stable defensive position in southern Malaya.

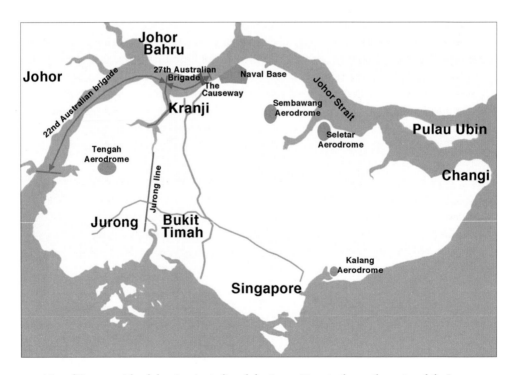

Map of Singapore Island showing Australian defensive positions to the north-west, and the Jurong defensive fall back line

Within a month of the loss of Force Z, from 12 January 1942 onwards, the Japanese Army and Navy Air Forces, now well established in northern Malaya, began a daylight-bombing blitz on Singapore Island. Two to three times a day, Japanese bombers in groups of 27 or 54 aircraft, crossed the skies above Singapore in tight formations. With only forty 3.7-inch heavy anti-aircraft guns at Singapore capable of firing at targets above 20,000 feet, the Japanese bombers had little to fear from British ground-fire.

The RAF was left with only two- to three-dozen fighters remaining available at Singapore, pitted against 400 Japanese fighters and bombers based in southern Thailand and Malaya. There were too few RAF fighters left to fight off the Japanese bomber escort fighters – let alone attack the bombers themselves. The dated Brewster Buffalo fighter had already been shown to be outclassed by the lighter and more nimble Japanese Zero fighter, and had little chance of winning a dogfight.

British commanders at Singapore hoped that sufficient RAF reinforcements would reach them to turn the tables on the Japanese. Fifty-one crated Hurricane fighters did indeed arrive on a supply convoy in middle-January 1942, but it was found that the heavy dust-filters (designed for service in the Middle East) and the weight of 12 guns and ammunition (instead of the usual eight) took 30 mph off the Hurricane's performance. However, unlike the Buffalo, they were still a match for the Zero over 20,000 feet – but proved disappointing at lower altitudes.

There were still simply too few Hurricanes to make a significant impact on the daily armada of Japanese aircraft freely over-flying Singapore. By 28 January, only 21 of the shipment of 51 Hurricanes were left available for operations – the others had been destroyed or were laid up for repair. All RAF bombers were withdrawn from Singapore to other safer locations, mostly in the Dutch East Indies.

British, Australian and Indian ground troops were forced to retreat southwards down the Malayan Peninsula towards Singapore in the face of the Japanese onslaught. Eventually they had fallen back to hold a small perimeter in Johor around the causeway over the Johor Strait, which separates the island of Singapore from the southern tip of Malaya.

The final withdrawal to Singapore came during the night of 30–31 January 1942. Making good use of their abundant motor transport, British, Australian and Indian troops sprang back from their defensive perimeter on the southern tip of Malaya over a distance of 20 miles in a single manoeuvre. The Japanese were taken by surprise and were unable to keep pace.

At 7 a.m., on the morning of 31 January 1942, the last Australians on the mainland along with the Gordon Highlanders retired over the causeway. They were followed later by a rearguard of 250 Argyll & Sutherland Highlanders – the last unit to leave Johor – who were led across the causeway by two pipers marching at their head.

Soon afterwards, at 8 a.m., naval depth-charges planted in the causeway were detonated, creating a 70-foot gap (which was only 4 feet deep at low water). At this time, the RAF determined to keep only eight Hurricanes and six of the last surviving Brewster Buffaloes at Singapore.

Shortly afterwards, General Yamashita's army reached the north bank of the Johor Strait and reconnaissance patrols soon ascertained that Lt. General Percival had divided his forces and spread them around the whole of Singapore's coastal rim. Singapore Island's defences were weakest in the north-west corner of the island, opposite the Johor Strait's narrowest stretch. The Japanese XXV Army battle-plan would pit the bulk of their forces against a small part of the defending force.

In the last days of January and the first week of February 1942, the main body of the 18th British Division, along with the 44th Indian Brigade, 7,000 Indian replacements, the 2/4th Machine Gun Battalion AIF and 1,900 Australian replacements sailed into Singapore from India and Australia with little interference from Japanese aircraft.

After the troop convoys arrived at Singapore, the ships were used to evacuate European women and children and RAF personnel. Convoy BM 11 had arrived on 29 January, and by the night of 30–31 January 1942, four of its large transport ships had left, carrying 5,000 evacuees and servicemen. On 6 February, three transports from convoy BM 12 also left Singapore, carrying 4,100 people. The writer's grandmother, Iva Macdonald, and her three sons, Gordon, Brian and Roderick Macdonald (the latter, the writer's father), were aboard one of these ships; whilst the writer's grandfather Charles Alexander Scott Macdonald, a prison officer at Changi Gaol, remained in Singapore as part of the civilian administration to preserve order.

The troop reinforcements that had now arrived brought Singapore's garrison to over 100,000 men. The Royal Marines rescued from *Prince of Wales* and *Repulse* were allocated to the beleaguered 250 surviving Argyll & Sutherland Highlanders, to boost their numbers.

Singapore Island itself was only 13 miles wide from north to south, and 27 miles east to west. There was some discord amongst British commanders as to how the garrison's troops should be set up to counter the imminent Japanese attack. If Lt. General Percival could predict where the Japanese would attack, he could mass his troops in that area and mount a robust defence.

Percival believed that the main Japanese attack would be made down the Johor River towards the east of Singapore Island. Others thought that the most likely place of attack would be the north-west of the island where the Johor Strait was at its narrowest. The Johor Strait north-east of Singapore Island was 5,000 yards wide, whereas west of the causeway it was only 800–2,000 yards wide.

Percival stationed the 8th Australian Division (of less than 3,000 men) on the north-west coast and sent the British 18th Division and Indian formations to the north-east coast. Intelligence reports to Percival had been exaggerated and many figures had simply been guessed at. Based on these flawed intelligence reports, Percival assessed that Japanese strength was approximately 150,000 men and 300 tanks. In fact Japanese troops numbered about 36,000 men.

These hopelessly inaccurate and exaggerated estimates combined to give an extremely misleading picture at Malaya Command HQ. Percival, who had always feared a landing on the south coast, placed most of his remaining troops on the south and south-east coast, leaving only a small central reserve force for deployment as the situation dictated. The garrison troops were spread right around the entire 70 miles of the island's coastline.

The sustained campaign and large advances had brought huge logistical problems for the Japanese, and – unknown to the British – Yamashita's troops were now running low on ammunition. He decided to attack Singapore quickly, after only one week's pause.

Yamashita assessed that because the British Naval Base was situated to the east of the causeway, the northern coast's defences would be strongest there. He was also aware of the powerful naval batteries and troop barracks near Changi on the north-east of the island. The attack had to come across the Johor Strait, and the obvious place to him was the north-west coast: it was the shortest crossing point and was also well away from the strongest parts of the British defences. A diversion was set up for the north-east coast of the island, to attract British attention there and away from the main north-west invasion site.

The Japanese assembled their landing craft in Johor – mostly they were collapsible motorboats that took 12 soldiers each. Barges and pontoons, which could each transport two- to three-dozen men, or a tank or a motor vehicle, were also made ready. The Japanese evacuated all civilians from a 20km-wide strip of land in Johor, north of Johor Strait, and Japanese troops started to mass well inland and away from the selected north-west crossing points. Yamashita assembled his artillery opposite Singapore Island with many of the heavier guns being sited on high ground behind Johor Bharu, from where they could fire at both west and east sides of the north coast of Singapore Island.

The British defence of the north coast caused grave concern to many. Drained mangrove swamps would impede any attacker, but were not an absolute barrier to a determined invader. However, they did cut down, or even eliminate many fields of fire for the defenders – who as they dug in, knew that it was unlikely that they would be able to hold their fronts against a determined Japanese assault. Japanese shelling from the mainland soon set fire to the British fuel dumps at the now-evacuated naval base, and a vast pillar of smoke rose ominously into the sky.

By 5 February 1942, Japanese artillery fire from Johor over the Johor Strait into Singapore Island had become noticeably heavier. British boat patrols operated in front of parts of the Northern Area and regular reconnaissance patrols from the British 18th Division were sent across the Johor Strait onto the Malayan mainland. Similarly, Japanese patrols were covertly landing on Singapore Island to probe British defences.

Once Yamashita was ready to launch the main attack, the Japanese diversion now went into operation as Imperial Guards drove lorries east from Johor Bharu towards dummy camps. On the evening of 7 February 1942, Imperial Guards landed 400 men in collapsible boats on the small island of Pulau Ubin (between mainland Johor and the north-east coast of Singapore Island). A British patrol on the island was forced to beat a hasty retreat.

The Japanese diversionary tactics and troop movements east of the causeway seemed so obvious that British Command's Intelligence Branch started to wonder whether they were in fact simply just a ruse, and suspicion grew that the attack may be directed at the north-west coast.

During 8 February 1942, Japanese artillery, supporting the Imperial Guards east of Johor Bharu, continued to fire towards Changi in the east, as part of their diversion. British counter-battery artillery work in the Northern Area returned fire with gusto. Nevertheless, Japanese shell-fire onto the north-west corner of the island – the true location of the impending assault – grew as the day progressed. Soon, all artillery fire was concentrated there in a bombardment. Luckily, Australian casualties were low, as the bursting shells lost much of their force in the soft ground of the swamp.

As Japanese gunfire reached a crescendo in the early evening, Australian scouts returned from the north-west with reports of large numbers of troops massing there. Australian commanders knew that a massed assault would quickly bypass the 3,000 Australian infantrymen dug-in on the north-west coast – it was hard to find fields of fire amid the mangroves and scrub.

The Australian scouts had in fact observed the entire 5th and 18th Japanese Divisions massing to assault Australian 22nd Brigade. But the small Japanese motorised boats, pontoons, and barges could only lift a total of 4,000 men with equipment at one time. The first 4,000-strong wave of the assault would not appreciably outnumber the thin line of 3,000 dug-in Australian defenders, and heavy Japanese losses were anticipated. However, each succeeding wave of 4,000 attackers would bring numbers that, by the time the planned 4th wave was landed at dawn, would far outnumber the Australian defenders.

During the evening of 8 February 1942, the Japanese bombardment lifted, and shaken Australian defenders rose from their water-logged pits, bracing themselves for the assault they knew would now follow. Soon after 10.30 p.m., dark shapes emerged from the gloom on the other side of the Johor Strait and began to close on the Australian positions. The Australians called down artillery fire with flares and telephone messages, but the artillery fire severed most of the buried telephone lines running to the Australian troops. With lines cut and flares hard to observe accurately at the rear artillery positions, little effective supporting-fire arrived when the alarm was raised.

On the Australian 22nd Brigade's right flank the 2/20th Battalion awaited the leading Japanese boats of the 5th Division. The battalion had three companies deployed along the Johor Strait to cover a front of 5,000 yards. One company, wearing headbands for identification, was deployed in the midst of the mangrove swamp, on the battalion's right flank. Further to the right, the swamps of Sungei Kranji were left undefended, as they were considered impassable. Along the front, swampy ground had made it difficult to dig trenches; so above-ground weapon pits protected only by timber beams had been built.

Japanese barges and craft moving across the Johor Strait were met with small arms fire from the Australians, and a barge loaded with explosives blew up, illuminating the scene and allowing Australian machine guns to target the now exposed craft. Few Japanese managed to get to the shore. However, the absence of firing coming from some points ashore revealed to the Japanese the undefended gaps in Australian defences. Japanese barges shied away from heavily-defended areas to assault the dark gaps from where no firing came.

The Japanese troops fired coloured flares to mark successful landings and started to press forward through the coastal mangroves into the jungle inshore. By midnight the Japanese were getting ashore in large numbers at the undefended points between the three companies of the Australian 22nd Brigade, and pressing on the Australian company flanks at either side of their landing points.

By 1 a.m., the Australian D Company had been ordered to retreat to a fall-back perimeter. By 1.30 a.m., having fired 10,000 rounds in three hours of fighting and now with little ammunition left, a Machine Gun Battalion was ordered to retreat. Japanese landing craft were locked together at the shore, and troops were jumping from barge to barge, forming up in company groups on the shore.

By daylight of 9 February 1942, the Australian 22nd Brigade had been swept off their Johor Strait defence perimeter, and new defensive lines were being established inland. Meantime, the Japanese consolidated their bridgehead – it is estimated that 13,000 troops crossed during the night, with another 10,000 landing just before dawn.

A 24-hour pause for consolidation in Japanese operations in the north-west corner of the island followed, between the mornings of 9 and 10 February 1942, as more troops and equipment were transferred over. This was the moment for a robust British counter-attack, but Percival, believing his intelligence reports that the Japanese had far greater numbers of troops still in reserve, was not prepared to shift troops away from the north-east and southern coasts – he still believed that fresh landings were imminent on other parts of the island. He was unaware that the bulk of the Japanese XXV Army was already ashore on the north-west coast.

The greatly-exaggerated reports of Japanese strength led Percival to believe that the Japanese had the ability in numbers to make more landings, and reports of Japanese shipping gathering at the Anambas Islands off the east coast would have coloured his thinking. Troops that might have been used to counter the Japanese bridgehead stood idle.

Meantime, the Japanese Imperial Guards were scheduled to attack the area between Sungei Kranji and the causeway to the east, on the evening of 9 February 1942. From there, they were to swing south-east to block the main route between Singapore town and Changi. The Japanese bombardment lifted at 8.30 p.m., and within half an hour, motor barges and launches were appearing out of the gloom, straight into the teeth of the 2/26th Battalion forward companies. Fierce and brutal hand-to-hand fighting took place in the swamps and the Japanese assault was successfully held at the main defence line 500 yards inland.

During the early hours of 10 February 1942, as the situation deteriorated rapidly with large numbers of Japanese now ashore in the north-west, orders were issued for a British withdrawal to a second defensive line – the Jurong Line, which ran from the north-west of the island to the south coast. At 12.50 a.m., Percival issued a plan for an inner defensive ring around Singapore town and Kalang aerodrome, which would apply if it proved impossible to hold the enemy at the Jurong Line. This inner defensive ring around Singapore is where the final battle for Singapore would take place.

Throughout the day, the Japanese forces started to fight their way south towards Singapore town, and a series of withdrawals by beleaguered units left neighbouring units exposed. Brigade and battalion commanders became wary of holding onto vulnerable positions once a front had begun to crumble.

The massed Japanese forces from the landings were to the north-west of the Jurong Line. With the Jurong Line becoming so vulnerable and individual units being forced to withdraw, Percival finally ordered the creation of a reserve brigade from 18th Division units. These were the first troops from coastal sectors in the Northern and Southern Area to be sent to aid the fighting in the western half of the island.

Early in the afternoon, Percival was advised that much of the Jurong Line had been lost, and he ordered a counter-attack in three stages. Churchill was keeping abreast of developments and complained that Singapore's garrison must greatly outnumber the Japanese on the island, and 'in a well-contested battle they should destroy them. There must at this stage be no thought of sparing the troops or population. Commanders and Senior Officers should die with their troops. The honour of the British Empire and of the British Army is at stake.'

During the early hours of 11 February 1942, aggressive Japanese attacks thwarted the counter-attack plans and then routed the reserve force. The planned second stage of the British counter-attack for dawn was cancelled, as Japanese infantry and tanks appeared out of the darkness. The Japanese took control of the strategically important crossroads at Bukit Panjang, before pushing south, down Woodlands Road until they reached roadblocks erected by the Argyll & Sutherland Highlanders. The leading Japanese tank in the column was disabled by the Argylls, but there were 50 more tanks behind. The roadblocks were brushed aside and the Japanese advance continued.

On 12 February 1942, the Japanese had consolidated their grip on Bukit Timah – the strategically important centre of Singapore Island, well on the way to Singapore town itself. Unknown to the British at this point, the outnumbered Japanese troops were badly stretched and alarmingly short of artillery ammunition. General Yamashita's plan now called for a concentration of his forces for a final thrust into Singapore Town, but in the interim, pressure would be maintained on the British perimeter.

By the afternoon of 13 February 1942, beleaguered British and Empire troops were fighting for survival and being forced back from their defensive lines. The situation was becoming hopeless and the seemingly impossible thought of defeat and capitulation had by now become a real possibility. That night, the Royal Navy decided to sail all its remaining 40 or so small vessels from Singapore, and evacuate staff officers, technicians, and other non essential personnel. Of those small ships that did leave that night, in darkness illuminated by the glow of fires ashore, most were sunk or captured the following day.

On the afternoon of 14 February 1942, advancing Japanese troops captured Alexandra Military Hospital, just 4 miles west of Singapore town, and went on a bloody rampage through it. A Loyals corporal was bayoneted on the operating table and other wounded service personnel were killed on the spot. Some patients were rounded up and taken outside – the immobile were bayoneted where they lay. About 150 patients and medical personnel were roped together in groups and bayoneted later that night.

Percival met with Singapore's chief Royal Engineer and the municipal Water Engineer to review the water supply situation. The bombing had broken many water mains pipes and there was a general water shortage. He was advised by the governor to surrender to alleviate the suffering being endured by the civilian population. Morale amongst troops and civilians alike was deteriorating, and several thousand stragglers from demolished infantry units roamed the back areas.

Dawn of 15 February 1942 revealed a desperate situation, as the Japanese continued to pound the fragile British perimeter. The damaged piped water supply was not expected to last into the next day, and it would take several days to restore the water supply. Ammunition was perilously low and there was no chance of a successful counter-attack. Percival accepted the advice of his senior officers to capitulate.

The British decided to ask the Japanese for a cease-fire from 4 p.m., that day. British officers and a civilian official went by car at 11.30 a.m., to meet with the Japanese commanders, but their car was stopped at a British roadblock and not allowed further. The British group continued on foot for 600 yards, carrying a Union Jack and a white flag.

After a short period, Colonel Sugita arrived from Japanese Army HQ to meet the British delegation. He made a series of demands and gave the British a large Japanese flag, which was to be flown at 4 p.m. over the Cathay Building in Singapore as a signal that Percival had agreed to meet Yamashita to finalise terms. The delegation was driven back towards British lines.

After meeting Percival at Fort Canning, Major Wild went to the top of the Cathay Building and flew the Japanese flag at 4 p.m., as instructed. Percival's' party then went by car, north up Bukit Timah Road, to meet the Japanese. When they met the Japanese officers at 5.15 p.m., Yamashita demanded that the British surrender immediately, as an attack was planned to go forward that evening against Singapore town itself. Percival asked to retain 1,000 men under arms to preserve order in the town. Yamashita banged his fist on the table and, speaking in

Lt. General Percival and the British surrender party, under a white flag, are taken to meet Japanese commanders. (IWM)

English, demanded: 'The time for the night attack is drawing near. Is the British Army going to surrender or not? Answer "Yes" or "No".'

Percival agreed and surrender terms were signed at 6.10 p.m. The two generals rose and shook hands.

On the morning of 16 February 1942, a Japanese officer called on the Singapore Governor and instructed him to assemble all European civilians at the nearby Padang next morning. The writer's grandfather, Charles Alexander Scott Macdonald, was among those. Around 3,000 European civilians would be interned at Changi gaol – grandfather included. British military leaders were told by the Japanese to march all the European personnel, including European officers of Asian troops, to Changi camp on 17 February 1942. That day, over 50,000 troops marched off to internment. It was the largest surrender of British troops in history.

As they entered Singapore town itself, Japanese troops embarked on a bloody revenge killing-spree against their old and hated enemies – the Chinese. These were innocent Chinese civilians; simple residents of Singapore, but nonetheless hated by the Japanese troops. The event came to be known as the 'Chinese Massacres'. Alleged Communists, Chinese Nationalists, criminals, members of secret sects and the like were rounded up, and after an often brutal interrogation were obliged to hand over all their personal possessions, rings, watches, and jewelry. They were then forced onto captured British lorries and driven to Tanjong Paga Wharf, where most were beheaded or bayoneted. Others were roped together and taken on barges out to sea where they were thrown overboard. The slaughter continued for 12 successive days, as boats from Singapore Harbour brought even more Chinese for execution.

Truckloads of Chinese detainees were driven off to beaches on the south coast, where the Chinese men were ordered to walk into the sea and were then machine-gunned by Japanese

Lt. General Yamashita Tomoyuki and Lt. General Percival discuss surrender terms at the Ford Works Building near the Bukit Timah Road, Singapore. (IWM)

Japanese troops march into Singapore after the Fall of Singapore and start the bloody Chinese massacres. (IWM)

guards. Mass executions were carried out, by rifle or machine gun, bayoneting or beheading by samurai sword. As many as 3,600 Chinese were gathered together at the Teluk Kurau English School: after interrogation they were taken by truck to the crest of a hill, where they were killed by rifle-fire, beheading or bayoneting. In another massacre just east of Changi, several hundred Chinese were beheaded. Their headless bodies were thrown into already-dug mass graves. The victims' heads were piled up in a waiting lorry and carted away. The next morning, throughout Singapore, the severed heads of the murdered Chinese were found on the tips of long bamboo stakes, lining the road to Changi gaol, as troops and civilian internees – including my grandfather – were marched there. Figures are vague and differ, but between 15,000 and 50,000 people were summarily executed by the Japanese invaders, in the most brutal and shocking manner. After the war, a British Military Court tried and sentenced the commanding general of the Chinese troops in Singapore – Lt. Gen Takuma Nishimura – and sentenced him to life imprisonment. A subsequent trial for other crimes by an Australian Military Court handed down a death sentence, and he was hanged on 11 June 1951.

Following the atomic bombs at Hiroshima and Nagasaki, Japan surrendered on 15 August 1945. The first Royal Navy warships reached and entered Singapore Harbour, on 3 September 1945, to resume colonial occupation.

Churchill would later comment: 'It never occurred to me for a moment that the gorge of the fortress of Singapore, with its splendid moat half a mile to a mile wide, was not entirely fortified against an attack from northward.

BOOK THREE

FORCE Z SHIPWRECKS OF THE SOUTH CHINA SEA

The massive wreck of the battleship HMS Prince of Wales lies upturned in 70 metres of water, 50 miles offshore of east Malaysia, in the South China Sea

CHAPTER ONE

THE WRECK OF HMS *PRINCE OF WALES*

HMS *Prince of Wales* is an immense ship. At 745 ft 1 in. long, she is almost 50 feet shorter than *Repulse* – but still 200 feet longer than the German World War I battleships at Scapa Flow. She sits broadside on to the tidal flow: this immense barrier in the path of the tide deflects water around her and agitates and lifts particles of sand and silt into the water column. As a result, on top of the upturned whaleback of the wreck, underwater visibility can be quite good and clear, but near the seabed, visibility can be reduced to 10–20 feet.

The wreck lies almost completely upside down in an average depth of 70 metres of water, on a soft sandy bottom. The least depth over her hull at her propellers is 50–55 metres. There is a near-vertical drop over the hull to the seabed of 15–20 metres. Although completely upside down, she has a list to port of 15–20 degrees. She rests on her port gunwale, whilst on the other, higher starboard side of the wreck, there is a gap of several metres from the gunwale to the seabed.

The wreck of *Prince of Wales* was designated as a 'Protected Place' in 2002 under The Protection of Military Remains Act 1986. This British legislation applies to British citizens and British controlled vessels and makes it *inter alia* an offence (a) for persons to tamper with, damage, move, remove or unearth the vessel and (b) for persons to enter any hatch or other opening to the interior.

(Although it is not forbidden to dive the wreck the legislation tries to achieve a 'look from the outside but don't touch or enter' policy. The legislation does not apply to non-UK persons, but it is hoped that divers of other nationalities will respect the UK legislation. These wrecks are very sensitive British war graves. Survivors and relatives of those that perished, or have died since from natural causes, deserve to be treated with dignity. The GPS coordinates for both wrecks have purposely not been published in this work.)

Prince of Wales turned turtle on the surface after the attack. As she sank, she struck the seabed and her uppermost works – her funnels, masts and rigging – were crushed as the far stronger armoured superstructure drove on behind into the seabed. She rolled over to port, until her port-side main deck for most of her length (bar the sweeping of her hull to bow and stern) settled on the seabed. She finally came to rest on her port rail almost totally upside

The Prince of Wales *now lies upturned on the seabed. Her bow, from A turret forward, is still suspended well above the seabed*

down, but with a list to her port side of 15–20 degrees. Over the years, sand has built up against the upturned port side of the hull, so that the main deck level is now well buried, from the stern all the way forward to the front of A turret. The main deck on the starboard side of the hull is raised up, several metres off the seabed.

The three starboard-side torpedo explosion holes are very visible along that side of the hull: one at the bow, one just under the bilge keel and above the (now upside down) armour belt, and the third at the aft end of the armour belt.

Bilge keels – thin strips of steel just a few feet high – run along either side of the main section of hull bottom, and were designed to give her flat bottom a cutting edge for maneuvering. On the hull bottom itself, docking keels – reinforced square strip boxes filled with oiled wood – can be seen. In a dry dock the hull would sit on these.

The ship would have carried a number of bells – and one of the smaller bells was spotted protruding from the sandy seabed under the forward part of the overhanging starboard-side main deck by British diver, Gavin Haywood, on a technical diving expedition to visit the wreck. Very properly, he reported its location to British military officials.

In 2002, a combined British military and civilian technical divers' grey funnel expedition, coordinated by Divex in Aberdeen, successfully recovered the bell, with the blessing and support of the Force Z Survivors Association. The bell was restored and presented for display by First Sea Lord and Chief of Naval Staff, Admiral Sir Alan West, to the Merseyside Maritime Museum in Liverpool.

The founding Secretary of the Force Z Survivors Association, the late Ken Byrne, advised the writer in one of our telephone conversations centering on the 2001 Tri-Services Expedition, that the ship's practice was that the large main bell was taken down from its mount as the ship

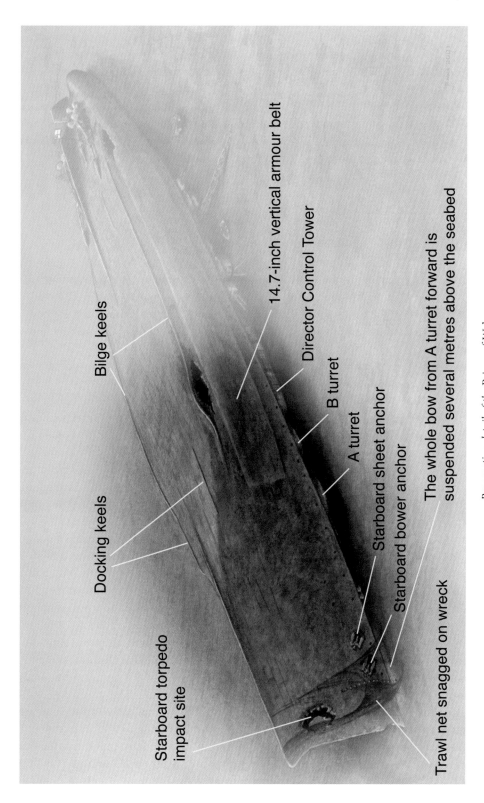

Bilge keels

14.7-inch vertical armour belt

Director Control Tower

B turret

A turret

Starboard sheet anchor

Starboard bower anchor

The whole bow from A turret forward is suspended several metres above the seabed

Docking keels

Starboard torpedo impact site

Trawl net snagged on wreck

Bow section detail of the Prince of Wales

went into action. The bell was then stored in its own cradle deep in the main superstructure of the ship. That bell will still be resting there in its cradle.

To this day, Royal Navy ships passing over the site of the Force Z ships perform a Remembrance Service.

For readers who wish to delve further into the technical details of how the ship was affected by the torpedo hits, how it flooded and sank and its conditiion today, reference should be made to *Death of a Battleship: a Re-analysis of the Tragic Loss of HMS* Prince of Wales by Garzke, Denlay and Dulin (2009) and the 2012 revision listed in the bibliography.

The wreck in detail

The Bow section

The almost-sheer stem of the bow drops down from 55 metres to the very tip of the upturned bow just a few metres off the seabed. Heavy gauge fishing nets, snagged on the wreck long ago, are still draped over the bow – with their floats still in line. The keel of the ship at the bow is narrow and sleek and gradually widens before flaring out at the citadel as the main section of the hull forms.

Both starboard anchors – the forward bower anchor and the aft sheet anchor – are still held snug in their hawses. The port-side bower anchor is also still secure in its hawse. A row of portholes – all closed with the glass still in place – dot along the hull just above (originally under) main deck level. A second row of portholes for the deck level below can be seen above.

Just a few metres back from the stem is the foremost of the three starboard-side torpedo explosion sites. Here a torpedo struck the hull almost directly beneath the forward of the two starboard anchors. A jagged hole some 7 metres in diameter was torn right through the ship, as the torpedo-blast blew clean through the hull and out through the port side, leaving a wide hole, right through the ship. The explosion also caused a horizontal crack from the hole forward to the stem itself. The damage from the explosion caused the immediate flooding of the two peak tanks and possibly the aviation and motor boat fuel tanks behind them in addition, although there was no explosion or fire. This torpedo explosion was well forward of the citadel, and in isolation, this hit was not a significant problem for the battleship.

On the port side of the hull, the superstructure and top hamper of the upturned battleship is well buried by a build up of sand over the years, to beyond main deck level, from the stern all the way forward to A turret. Forward of A turret, the narrowing sweep of the hull towards the bow causes the port-side main deck to rise clear of the sand. The result is that the whole bow section forward of A turret is suspended 2–4 metres off the seabed in free water, despite the ravages of her time underwater, by the incredible strength of her construction. On the higher starboard side, the main deck sits several metres off the seabed, creating a dark, brooding and overhanging chasm.

The top of the foremost quadruple 14-inch A turret is also buried in the sand, up to the level of the massive starboard-side gun barrels. When the writer visited the wreck in 2001 on the Tri-Services Expedition, all four 14-inch main gun barrels were visible, seemingly lying on top of

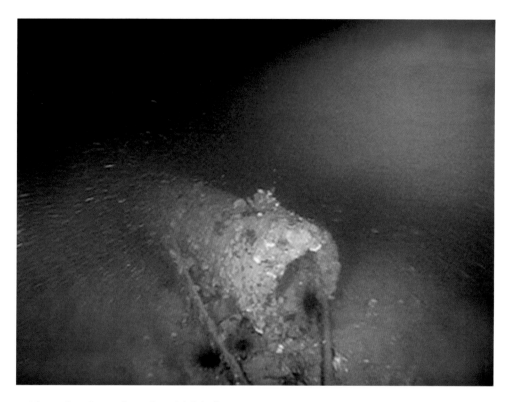

The starboard 14-inch gun barrel (of 4) of A turret rests just above the seabed, under the overhanging foredeck. © Guy Wallis

the sandy seabed with the starboard-side barrels slightly higher. In the thorough and excellent *Death of a battleship: a Re-analysis of the Tragic Loss of HMS Prince of Wales*, by Garzke, Denlay and Dulin (members of the SNAME Marine Forensics Committee) in 2009, it was reported that only the three starboard-side 14-inch gun barrels of A turret were visible. The outer starboard-side barrel was completely clear of the seabed, with the other two barrels progressively covered by sand. The outmost port-side barrel was, at that time, completely buried. The strong monsoon currents continuously scour under the hull, at times excavating the sand underneath the bow, and at other times infilling.

By venturing under the overhanging main deck, it is possible to locate A turret, the armoured base of B turret barbette, and the massive director control tower superstructure abaft it. B turret was a superfiring twin 14-inch turret – that is, it was situated higher and abaft the foremost quadruple A turret. Consequently, being a higher superfiring turret, as the ship is now upside down, B turret is now far lower down than A turret, and is well buried deep in the seabed. Neither of the B turret gun barrels are visible.

It is the immense strength of the armoured citadel bulkhead, the horizontal armoured decks and the vertical side armour belts, allied to the armoured forward gun turrets, barbettes and armoured castle superstructure, that has enabled the bow to hang above the seabed, defying gravity and corrosion for more than 70 years. A less-heavily constructed ship – such as a merchant ship – would have collapsed long ago. However, there are

The wreck of the Prince of Wales with the citadel area highlighted

now visible signs that the last 20 metres or so of the front section of the ship, forward of the citadel, is starting to sag. Eventually, in time, the bow section of *Prince of Wales* will succumb to the elements and collapse, forward of the citadel, and come to resemble the German World War I battleships at Scapa Flow. There, albeit due to the attention of salvers (who removed the athwartships armoured bulkheads of the citadels, weakened the structure, and hastened collapse), all three battleships have collapsed bow sections forward of the citadel. However, also like the German battleships at Scapa Flow, the armoured citadel section of *Prince of Wales* will still be structurally sound for many decades to come.

The Midships section

The armour belt is the dominant feature of the hull side. This 14.7-inch-thick armour belt runs from just forward of A turret, all the way back to just aft of Y turret, and would give protection against the shells from other battleship main guns. It ran down the side of the ship into the water and would take and easily withstand the impact of a relatively small torpedo warhead.

Of the three starboard-side torpedo hits in the final wave of the attack, moving aft from the bow, the first was close to the stem of the bow itself. The site of the second torpedo impact can be seen, not far along the main vertical armour belt, almost directly under (now above) B turret. There is a large hole in the thin steel of the unarmoured bottom section of the ship's starboard hull, between the belt and the prominent bilge keel. When the torpedo struck, a plume of oil and water shot up the side of the ship here. The blast from this torpedo strike opened up a crumpled hole some 6 metres across and 4 metres high, directly into the inner lower sections of the ship.

Had *Prince of Wales* not been listing to port, then this torpedo would have struck the 14.7-inch-thick vertical armour belt and been easily dealt with. However, the list to port had rolled the ship slightly over and raised the starboard side of the hull up in the water. This also raised the unarmoured underbelly of the ship (usually protected from torpedo attack by its depth in the water) into shallower water. The Japanese torpedoes were set to run at a depth of 6 metres but, with the elevation of the starboard side, the torpedo struck at the very bottom of the main vertical armour belt, exploding into the unarmoured starboard-side hull bottom.

The armour plating here is absolutely unscathed by the torpedo explosion, although the bottom plate of the armour belt is now angled inwards into the hull. The blast did not do any damage to the unyielding armour belt itself – the only evidence of the effect of the explosion on the belt is that the bottom plate is out of line.

It may be that the torpedo struck the very bottom of the raised belt, exploded, and perhaps damaging the internal belt supporting structure, knocked the bottom plate of the armour belt inwards and out of line. The blast could have then been deflected by the armour belt downwards and punched into the unarmoured ship's hull below. Alternatively, the explosion could have occurred completely below the armour belt, in the ship's soft hull, compromising the armour belt support structure and causing it to go out of line. I will leave that point for others better qualified to debate and resolve.

The normally straight three-foot high, thin bilge keel (which ran along either side of the middle section of the flat bottom of the hull) has been bent and buckled around the site of the

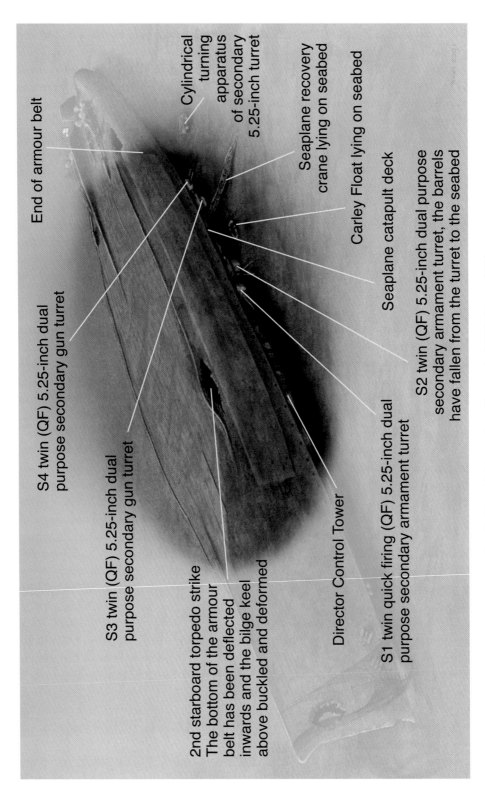

End of armour belt

Cylindrical turning apparatus of secondary 5.25-inch turret

Seaplane recovery crane lying on seabed

Carley Float lying on seabed

Seaplane catapult deck

S2 twin (QF) 5.25-inch dual purpose secondary armament turret, the barrels have fallen from the turret to the seabed

S4 twin (QF) 5.25-inch dual purpose secondary gun turret

S3 twin (QF) 5.25-inch dual purpose secondary gun turret

2nd starboard torpedo strike The bottom of the armour belt has been deflected inwards and the bilge keel above buckled and deformed

Director Control Tower

S1 twin quick firing (QF) 5.25-inch dual purpose secondary armament turret

Detail of the midships section of the wreck of HMS Prince of Wales

explosion. A hole this size directly into the innards of the ship would have caused significant flooding.

The side-protection system inner voids in this area had earlier been flooded in an attempt to counter the port list; and the outer voids had also been flooded when it became clear that the first phase of counter-flooding had not been effective. As part of the counter flooding, washrooms on the lower deck and living spaces on the middle deck had all been flooded with salt water and oil – and this mixture formed the plume of water and oil seen rising skywards after the strike.

But essential though the flooding had been, incompressible water in these rooms and voids prevented them from functioning as designed in the side-protection system, and allowed much of the energy from the torpedo explosion to be vented into the ship itself. It is a sad fact that the torpedo struck immediately beside the bottom of the armour belt – it may even have detonated on the bottom of the belt itself. If the list had been just a few feet less, the torpedo would have struck the armour belt – which would have taken the hit without difficulty.

Prince of Wales carried four twin 5.25-inch dual-purpose secondary armament gun turrets on either side, designated on the starboard side (moving aft from the bow): 'S1', 'S2', 'S3' and 'S4'. On each side of the ship, two superfiring turrets (S1 & S2 on the starboard side) were situated relatively close together at the base of the forward main superstructure. Two further superfiring twin 5.25-inch turrets (S3 & S4 on the starboard side) were situated close together on either side of the after superstructure.

The foremost twin 5.25-inch secondary armament turret on the starboard side – S1 – is well clear of the sand and has its guns still in situ. The barrels point off the starboard bow. Just aft of it, at seabed level, the nearby secondary twin 5.25-inch gun turret – S2 – is partly buried in the sand, its casemate surround and most of its mounting still exposed. The two 5.25-inch barrels of S2 have been pulled out of their mounts in the turret and lie beside it on the seabed. The S2 turret, now at seabed level, is trained forward, pointing off the starboard bow at minimum elevation – in a similar orientation to the S1 5.25-inch turret. These guns would have been in action during the final starboard-side torpedo attack, and with the port-list raising the starboard side of the ship, they would have been required to be almost fully depressed to train on the low-flying Japanese torpedo-bombers coming in on their bombing runs at a height of 35 metres. Unlike the stern 5.25-inch guns, the forward 5.25-inch guns still had electrical power to train and elevate or depress during this attack. Several Carley floats also lie on the seabed near S2 turret.

As with *Repulse*, the main forward section of superstructure was separated from the smaller stern superstructure by a wide section of open flat main deck. Athwartships, across this open section of deck, ran the seaplane catapult tracks for launching the seaplanes off to either side of the ship. At either side of the open catapult deck space, at the front of the stern superstructure and one deck up, stood the rotating cranes used for recovering the seaplanes and small boats onto the ship. A long section of the starboard aircraft/boat crane lies on the seabed, projecting directly out from the wreck.

Immediately aft of the catapult deck and crane, the S3 5.25-inch turret is located, at the very front of the after superstructure. It is now partially buried in the sand with its casemate and part of the mounting exposed, but with no guns visible.

A diver hovers beside the second (from bow) starboard torpedo explosion site. Note the straight edge of the undamaged bottom of the armour belt below. © Guy Wallis

Inverting the previous image of the site of the second (from bow) starboard-side torpedo hit (so that the image is as the ship would have been on the surface), the straight edge of the armour belt now above is obvious. © Guy Wallis

A diver looks into the second (from bow) torpedo impact site. The bottom of the armour belt is beneath the nose of the scooter, and the front of the bilge keel can be seen starting towards the top of the image. © Guy Wallis

The roof of the aftmost 5.25-inch turret – S4 – is at seabed level. Its guns point to starboard and are depressed to minimum elevation, left as they were after firing at incoming Japanese aircraft as the gun-crew was finally released to abandon ship.

Lying on the seabed nearby, is what appears to be the inverted working chamber for a 5.25-inch secondary gun turret – the section that would have led down below decks into the ship. The roller ring around it, on which the turret would have rotated, can be seen.

In places along either side of the hull the unarmoured hull plates have detached and become separated from the far stronger armour belt plates. This indentation may be a natural consequence of the degradation of the wreck over time or may be a legacy from near miss bomb explosions during the battle itself.

The Stern section

The third (from bow) torpedo impact site from the final starboard-side wave of torpedo attacks is about 10 metres wide and several metres high, and is situated in the thin section of the ship's side, just at the end of the armour belt. In comparison to the other two torpedo hits, this damage is located much higher on the hull side, as a consequence of the ship settling by the stern following the flooding of after spaces along the port-side prop-shaft tunnel, after the very first wave of the attack, 40 minutes earlier.

As with the second (from bow) torpedo impact damage, if the torpedo had struck the armour belt, this would have easily handled the force of the explosion. But the torpedo struck just aft of the armour belt – and caused massive damage well into the ship, with decks visible inside the hole.

Both massive starboard-side propellers are still in situ – but the site of this third torpedo explosion was close to the supporting bracket for the free section of the outer starboard propeller shaft. The force of the blast destroyed the supporting bracket struts for the free section of shaft. This free section of shaft (with its propeller still attached) is now angled upwards and rests jammed over the inner starboard shaft. When the ship was fighting, once the supporting strut was damaged, the enormous weight of the shaft and still-turning propeller would have caused the shaft and prop to fall downwards, and as it turned, to jam itself in its present position. Now, with the ship being upside down, the outer shaft appears to rest above the inner shaft. The blades of the outer propeller show damage to their edges, which indicate it was still turning when it was jammed into its present position.

A prominent raised flat keel plate leads astern from the main hull on the centre line of the ship's bottom to the massive single rudder. This still stands upright in place, but is at an angle of about 20 degrees. A direct legacy of the battle, it is still in the position it was jammed in during the first wave of the attack, when the first port-side torpedo hit, destroyed electrical power in the stern part of the ship, and caused both steering motors to fail. The ship was left unmanoeuvrable and unable to turn her rudder – only able to make a fixed slow turn to port.

Only one of the two port-side propellers is still in place – the port inner propeller. The port outer propeller is missing, having detached itself with a section of its shaft during the initial stages of the action, and fallen to the seabed. Debris from the damage to the outer prop entered the inner propeller race, damaging the inner propeller and putting it out of action.

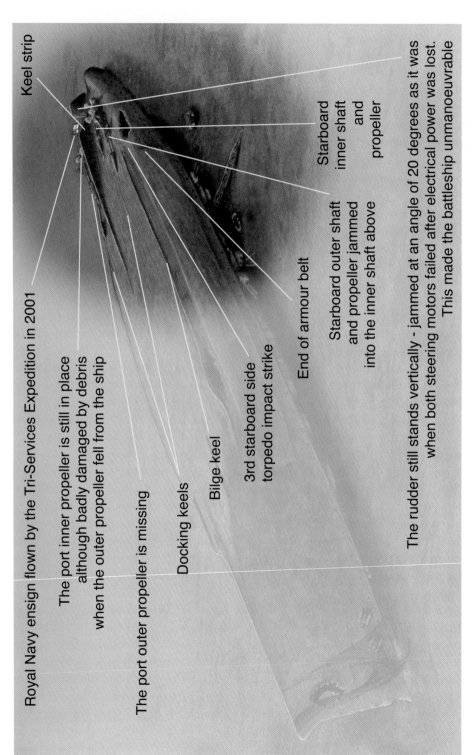

Keel strip

Royal Navy ensign flown by the Tri-Services Expedition in 2001

The port inner propeller is still in place although badly damaged by debris when the outer propeller fell from the ship

The port outer propeller is missing

Docking keels

Bilge keel

3rd starboard side torpedo impact strike

End of armour belt

Starboard outer shaft and propeller jammed into the inner shaft above

Starboard inner shaft and propeller

The rudder still stands vertically - jammed at an angle of 20 degrees as it was when both steering motors failed after electrical power was lost. This made the battleship unmanoeuvrable

Stern section detail

Starboard-side outer prop of HMS Prince of Wales *and the shaft of the inner prop in the background. Note damage to blades caused by it striking the inner shaft and associated debris whilst still turning. © Author's collection.*

The large hole blasted into the hull near the port outer propeller by the first torpedo strike is clearly visible, with a section of the stern tube protruding from the hull and now angled downwards. The hull here has split along the base of the armour belt to expose some of the inner web frames that supported the stern tube. These are deformed, as a result of the torpedo explosion.

Far below at seabed level, the hull sweeps round towards its narrow stern. The quadruple 14-inch Y turret main armament is well buried under the hull, and is not visible. Portholes still with their glass in place are dotted around the hull as it sweeps back.

As part of the 2001 British Tri-Services Expedition to the wreck, under the leadership of the then Major Guy Wallis, the military divers flew a Royal Navy Ensign (provided by the Royal Navy) near the stern, securing it to a starboard shaft and floating it with buoys. When the writer returned to the wreck in 2005, the ensign was still in situ, having been kept flying by successive groups of visiting divers.

The wreck of the battlecruiser HMS Repulse lies well heeled over on her port side in 55 metres of water, 50 miles offshore from the east coast of Malaysia, in the South China Sea

CHAPTER TWO

THE WRECK OF HMS *REPULSE*

HMS *Repulse* is a big, big ship. A Renown-class battlecruiser, built during World War I, her overall length from stem to stern was 794 ft 1.5 in. – more than 200 feet longer than the World War I König-class German High Seas Fleet battleships that lie at the bottom of Scapa Flow. She had a beam of 90 feet and displaced 27,200 long tons; fully loaded for combat her displacement increased to 32,220 long tons.

As she sank, she quickly rolled over onto her port side and plunged down to the seabed in a depth of 55 metres. She now rests on a clean sandy seabed more than 120 nautical miles north of Singapore and 50 miles off the land. She is well heeled over, resting on her port side, with her main deck at an angle of almost 40 degrees – almost but not quite, turned turtle like the *Prince of Wales*. The shallowest upturned starboard side is at a depth of 38 metres.

The hull of the ship, being a strongly built and armoured warship that has only been submerged since World War II, is in very good condition. Contrast this against the World War I German cruisers and battleships at Scapa Flow, which have been submerged since 1919. In the 1980s they were in reasonable condition, but the extra decades of submersion have seen recent and rapid accelerating decay and collapsing. Eventually, in the decades to come, *Repulse* will meet the same fate.

The underwater visibility on *Repulse* is far better than that on her Force Z colleague *Prince of Wales*, as a result of her flush orientation to the prevailing monsoon currents, which tend to sweep along her from bow to stern, sweeping away any silt or sedimentary debris. As a result, the underwater visibility is usually excellent, with anything up to 200 feet.

Sixty years after her sinking, in 2002, the wreck site of *Repulse* (along with *Prince of Wales* and several other famous shipwrecks) was designated as a 'Protected Place' by The Protection of Military Remains Act 1986. When wrecks such as *Repulse* and *Prince of Wales* are designated as a Protected Place under the act, this makes it an offence to conduct unlicensed diving or salvage operations, to tamper with, damage, remove or unearth the vessel, or enter any hatch or other opening. Diving is not forbidden, but is permitted on a 'look but don't touch' basis. As *Repulse* and *Prince of Wales* lie in international waters, the Protection of Military Remains Act applies to British nationals and to British-controlled ships – but non-British divers and ships are not controlled by the terms of the act. It is hoped that all divers however will respect the terms of the legislation and the feelings of survivors and relatives of those who perished in relation to these two very sensitive Britsh war graves.

Survivors from the battle described five torpedo hits on *Repulse*: four on the port side and one on the starboard side. Damage to the wreck from one of the four port-side hits can be seen abeam of the rear turret, and damage from a second can be seen close to her propellers. The port-side midships section of the wreck however is buried in the seabed, and the location of the hits there cannot be confirmed. The starboard-side hit was amidships on the torpedo bulge, and the hole caused by the torpedo exploding is a clearly visible feature on this uppermost side of the wreck. It is tragic to recall the report from the time which told how one officer, whilst abandoning ship, mistimed his jump and fell back into this hole and perished.

Her two uppermost starboard-side propellers were salvaged a long time ago and are missing from the wreck.

The wreck in detail

The Bow section (stem to B turret)

In the immediate run up to World War I, Admiral Lord Fisher had presented his requirements for a new version of his battlecruiser concept to the Director of Naval Construction. He wanted new battlecruisers with a long, high, flared bow – like that on the old pre-dreadnought HMS *Renown* – and 15-inch main armament guns in twin turrets. The flared bow Fisher demanded is still one of the dominant features of this wreck: a beautiful piece of exquisite engineering. At the very tip of the flared bow, the jack staff tripod support – which would have held her forward flagpole and on which her battle ensign was hoisted as she went into action against the Japanese bombers – still stands in situ. It can clearly be seen in the wartime photograph of the ship below.

Starboard view of HMS Repulse. *The oval Carley float abreast the bridge superstructure is still on the wreck*

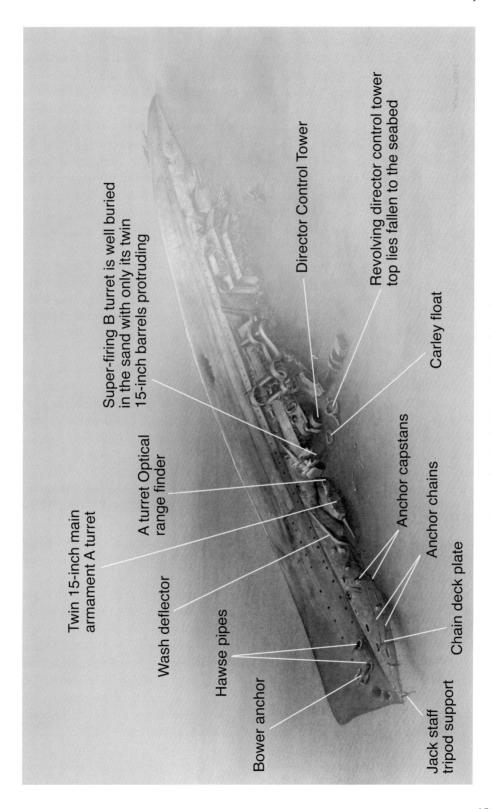

Twin 15-inch main armament A turret

Super-firing B turret is well buried in the sand with only its twin 15-inch barrels protruding

A turret Optical range finder

Director Control Tower

Revolving director control tower top lies fallen to the seabed

Wash deflector

Carley float

Hawse pipes

Anchor capstans

Bower anchor

Anchor chains

Chain deck plate

Jack staff tripod support

Bow section detail of the wreck of HMS Repulse

Both her uppermost starboard-side and lower port-side anchors are still held snug in their hawses. The anchor chains run back through hawse pipes to deck plates and then run along the now-vertical deck to anchor capstans, before disappearing below deck to their chain lockers. Like all Royal Navy capital ships of World War I, she was originally fitted out with three bow anchors: two main 'bower anchors' (one either side of the hull and cabled for immediate use), and a third 'sheet anchor' (a spare anchor), which was a smaller, different design to the main two, and did not have its own capstan. The cable for the sheet anchor simply ran out from the chain locker and along the deck – it did not have a substantial deck plate for its chain like the two other main anchors. The sheet anchor was not required for immediate use, but was a spare for deployment should one of the chains for a main bower anchor break. The third sheet anchor on *Repulse* was dispensed with in time, presumably to save weight as other new items were added, increasing her weight. The Royal Navy continued to fit a third sheet anchor to its capital ships through to the end of World War II.

In front of the foremost twin 15-inch turret (A turret), is an elevated wash deflector, which ran athwartships in front of A turret and then angled backwards to either side of the deck. The wash deflector was designed to protect personnel working on deck around the forward section of the ship from the often dangerous amounts of water that could sweep the deck as she dipped and burrowed in difficult seas – it was designed to take any wash coming over the foredeck and deflect it off the deck to sea.

Although she had a flared bow, *Repulse* – particularly when fully laden – ran quite deeply in the water, and in even a moderate sea, water could come over her bow. British Pathé have some wonderful footage of *Repulse* in moderate seas, moving at speed and firing her main guns. She runs deep in the water, and as she buries her bow in the seas, a massive bow splash billows up, obliterating the foredeck back to A turret. Huge amounts of white water cascade off the side of the wreck at the wash deflector.

The foremost A turret itself is half buried by a build up of sand against the over hanging main deck – only the topmost half of the starboard-side 15-inch gun barrel rises clear of the seabed, pointing dead ahead. The barbette – the armoured cylinder of steel housing all the critical machinery to turn the turret and fire the gun, and accommodating the shell and cordite charge transfer hoists – ran from the turret gun room down through many deck-levels into the bowels of the ship to the forward magazine. Only a small section of A barbette rises clear of the deck, underneath the turning part of the turret, the gun room.

Before the dreadnought era, battleships had no centralized fire control and each gun was fired independently of the others. The new dreadnoughts and the later battlecruiser developments had the latest in rangefinding techniques, sighting and fire control, and all eight guns in a broadside could for the first time be aimed and fired by one gunnery control officer positioned in the fire control tower (conning tower or foretop), or in the spotting top well up the foremast. Each individual turret, however, still had its own large horizontal integral optical rangefinder situated at the back of the turret. This rectangular device projected out horizontally at either side of the rear of the turret, and would allow individual firing of the guns if central fire control broke down. At the back of A turret, the starboard-side of the large rangefinder still projects outwards from the turret.

Immediately behind A turret, the super-firing B turret is largely buried in the sand. Firing over the top of A turret, it stood higher, with more of its barbette exposed above deck.

Consequently, being higher, it is now buried deeper in the sand than A turret. The two 15-inch barrels of B turret have been swung out to starboard during the final stages of the battle, presumably to counter her port list as she filled with water. The barrels of A turret and Y turret at the stern, however, are not swung out to starboard – they point directly forward and astern. None of the references that the writer reviewed commented on this aspect – but perhaps the damage from the final round of attacks destroyed coordinated training of all turrets simultaneously, and B turret was rotated alone to swing her barrels out to starboard. They now emerge from the sandy seabed from the buried turret, pointing upwards at the same 40-degree angle as her main deck.

Carley floats – rigid life rafts – were secured at many places to the bridge superstructure. These rigid Carley floats were made from a length of copper tubing divided into waterproof sections, bent into an oval ring and then surrounded by cork or kapok, and covered with a layer of waterproofed canvas. The raft was rigid and could remain buoyant even if the waterproof outer or individual compartments were punctured. When Captain Tennant gave the order for everyone to come on deck, he ordered the Carley floats cast loose. But *Repulse* went down so quickly – in just 11 minutes from the first torpedo strike – that many Carley floats appear not to have been cut free from their lashings before she went. Several of these can still be found dotted around the wreck – perhaps some became snagged as she went under or were carried down by the suction of her passing. Many archive photos of *Repulse* afloat show that a number of Carley floats were secured against the sheer forward section of the bridge superstructure. Today, one Carley float lies flat on the seabed beside B turret, and

The 15-inch guns of A and B turrets. HMS Repulse *with the revolving top of the director control tower immediately aft and above the roof of B turret*

Above: The twin 15-inch guns of B turret. To the left of the picture the rangefinder at the rear of half-buried A turret can be seen. © Guy Wallis

Below: A diver hangs in midwater beside the twin 15-inch gun barrels of B turret. © Guy Wallis

Looking down the twin 15-inch gun barrels of B turret from the turret itself. The rangefinder and back of A turret can be seen to the right of the picture. © Guy Wallis

a second Carley float is still secured in place on the flat section of superstructure, just aft of the starboard-side triple 4-inch anti-aircraft gun platform. The latter can clearly be seen in the previous archive photograph of *Repulse*.

The armoured conning tower – or director control tower – was situated immediately behind B turret. The top of the director control tower held a revolving chamber with a circular base, which had optical rangefinders protruding from either side. From here, all the guns were directed, controlled, and fired.

The conning tower was a feature of most battleships and cruisers from the late 19th century until the early years of World War II. Although when not in action, a capital ship would be navigated from the bridge, the conning tower was located at the front end of the superstructure and was a heavily-armoured cylinder, varying on different ships from 4.5 inches to 12 inches thick, with tiny slit windows on three sides providing a field of view for officers during battle. It was fitted out, to allow navigation during battle, with engine order telegraphs, speaking tubes, telephones and helm. Royal Navy analysis of World War I combat revealed that officers were unlikely to use the conning tower during battle, preferring the open superior views of the unarmoured open bridge. Older Royal Navy ships that were reconstructed with new superstructures had their heavily-armoured conning tower replaced with lighter structures.

A diver swims past the starboard side of the bridge superstructure. At the bottom of the photograph can be seen the triple 4-inch gun abreast the bridge. Only one barrel remains in place. To the right, a Carley float can be seen, still lashed in place. © *Guy Wallis*

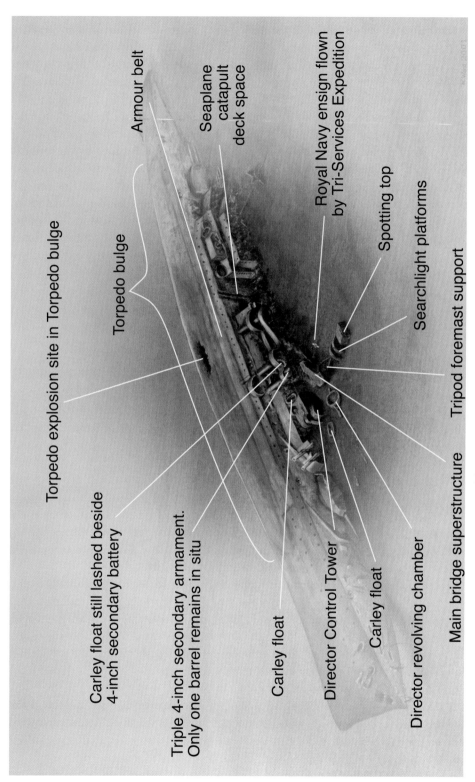

Armour belt

Seaplane
catapult
deck space

Royal Navy ensign flown
by Tri-Services Expedition

Spotting top

Searchlight platforms

Tripod foremast support

Torpedo explosion site in Torpedo bulge

Torpedo bulge

Carley float still lashed beside
4-inch secondary battery

Triple 4-inch secondary armament.
Only one barrel remains in situ

Carley float

Director Control Tower

Carley float

Director revolving chamber

Main bridge superstructure

Midships detail of the wreck of HMS Repulse

Lying fallen to the seabed near the director control tower is the circular revolving top section of the tower – from where all the guns could be trained, elevated and fired in action. The large rectangular optical rangefinder is still set on its top at the rear. When the crew of the tower received an indication of the enemy target from the captain via 'the captain's sight' device, the revolving top section of the tower was trained round until the target selected by the captain could be seen. This gave the bearing of the target, and this was then sent to the guns electrically. The guns were then all trained on the same bearing as the director control tower. The bearing of the target was also sent by the director control tower to the transmitting station: the gunnery nerve centre of the ship, deep down inside the citadel and protected by its horizontal and vertical armour. Here, the 'aim-off' – or additional training movement required to hit the enemy – would be calculated and sent to the guns, which were then pointed in slightly a different direction to the director control tower. The Admiralty Fire Control Table also sent to the guns the movement in elevation required by the range (calculated initially by optical rangefinders and latterly by radar) to the enemy.

The guns were now pointed and elevated correctly, and ready to be fired by the director layer. The director layer sat in the front position of the revolving top section of the tower that now lies on the seabed, looking through a telescopic sight ('the director sight') at the enemy. Beside the director layer sat the director trainer, whose job it was to train the tower on the target and keep it trained as the target moved. As the guns became loaded and ready to be fired, individual 'gun ready' lamps lit up in the transmitting station. As soon as all the 'gun ready' lamps showed 'READY', the transmitting station pressed a button on the Admiralty Fire Control Table, and this rang a gong in the director control tower. When this was heard, the director layer pressed his trigger as soon as he was on the target, and all the guns were fired simultaneously by an electric current.

The Midships section

With the ship lying well over at an angle of 40 degrees, much of the upper parts of the bridge superstructure, from where the vessel would be fought in action, have now been engulfed by the shifting sands of the seabed. The uppermost starboard side of B turret barbette and the massive smooth, sheer armoured superstructure aft of it are visible.

Abreast of the bridge superstructure – and originally two deck levels above the main deck – can be found one of the four triple-barreled secondary 4-inch gun platforms. Only one of its three barrels is still in place, and this points out over the starboard side in the position it was last fired in action, during the final moments of the battle. With the cant of the ship, this starboard-side triple 4-inch gun now points obliquely towards the surface. The infilling encroachment of the sandy seabed has covered the upper works of the ship so much that this starboard-side gun is now found not far above the seabed (there was another triple 4-inch secondary gun mount on the port side of the bridge superstructure, but this is well buried beneath the sand and superstructure on the low side of the ship). A quadruple Mark II mounting for the 0.5-inch Vickers Mark III machine gun was set in a circular platform adjacent.

Just aft of this 4-inch gun platform, a Carley float is still lashed in place beside it. Such

Above: The author approaches a Carley float abreast the bridge superstructure HMS Repulse. *© Guy Wallis*

Below: Amidst snagged fishing nets, suspended on buoys, a diver approaches a secondary 4-inch gun barrel on the starboard side of the bridge superstructure. © Guy Wallis

The author beside the Royal Navy Ensign just flown by the Tri-Services Expedition on the spotting top of HMS Repulse. *The massive bulk of the horizontal hull looms in the background. © Guy Wallis*

was the speed that *Repulse* sank that this float and many others were not released in time. The float can be seen bottom right in the underwater photograph on page 144. On main deck level, just below and aft, a circular gun platform for one of her 8-barreled 2-pounder 'Pom-Pom' anti-aircraft guns can be seen. Aft of that, a circular gun mount for her smaller calibre weapons can be found.

The towering superstructure with its sheer, smooth walls runs away into the sand with square windows ringed around it and other platforms. A tripod mast then runs out to searchlight platforms and the armoured spotting top, which again has small square windows set in it. It was here that service personnel flew a White Ensign during the 2001 Tri-Services Expedition.

Just aft of the battle bridge were situated two large funnels – but little trace of them can now be seen on the wreck. Made of far lighter steel, they will have been crumpled and will now be well corroded away and buried in the sand that has built up against the wreck.

Aft of the main superstructure, a clear space divides it from the after superstructure. This space is from where the Walrus seaplanes were launched, and the catapult tracks can be seen in situ running from one side of the hull to the other. A rotating crane was set on either side of the deck here for recovering the seaplane (and ship's boats), after it had landed near *Repulse* after flight.

The most visible feature of the hull itself here is the large torpedo blister, which is integral to the hull itself and runs for much the length of the hull. In the middle, a Japanese torpedo has blasted a large hole into it, just aft of the bridge superstructure (see photograph below).

A pronounced bilge keel – a thin strip of steel some 3–4 feet high – runs along the bottom edge of the hull on each side. This was designed to give the flat bottom of the vessel a cutting edge for manoeuvering.

Torpedo impact site on the uppermost starboard torpedo bulge. © Guy Wallis

The Stern section

Separated from the forward main bridge superstructure by the Walrus seaplane launch area, lies the after superstructure, dotted with portholes. The main mast runs out from this superstructure and now lies flat on the seabed. Halfway up it, is the star-shaped platform base for the after spotting position. This base also acted as a spreader to marshal standing rigging, and a lot of the rigging is jumbled up at its base, covered in sea life.

Just aft of the main mast, the superstructure steps down in three levels to the quarterdeck, and many mixed calibre gun platforms are dotted around here. The aft-facing triple 4-inch gun platforms here are largely buried in the sand, and a starboard-side single 4-inch gun platform is situated abreast the main mast. Just aft of this can be located an 8-barreled 2-pounder 'Pom-Pom' anti-aircraft gun – the 'Chicago Piano'. Beside this 'Pom-Pom' gun lies another Carley float not cut loose in time – half wedged underneath the gun itself.

The superstructure drops down to a cut-away quarterdeck, which is one deck level lower than the main foredeck forward. Here on the quarterdeck is situated the twin 15-inch Y turret. Like A and B turrets at the bow, Y turret has a large optical rangefinder projecting at either side at the back of the gun room. It is clearly visible in the photograph below. The gun room is now half buried in the encroaching sand, with only the topmost starboard-side 15-inch barrel now visible.

The quarterdeck sweeps back for a long way, to a seemingly slender, delicate stern – the deck being studded here and there with twin mooring bollards.

Repulse was powered by four massive propellers: needed to push this vast ship to her design speed of 31 knots. The free section of propeller shaft and brackets for the two higher starboard-side propellers are visible, however the propellers are no longer on the wreck, having been removed some considerable time ago, long before she became a Protected Place. The two lower propellers remain on the wreck.

Stern view of HMS Repulse *showing Y turret and triple 4-inch secondary armament on the decks above*

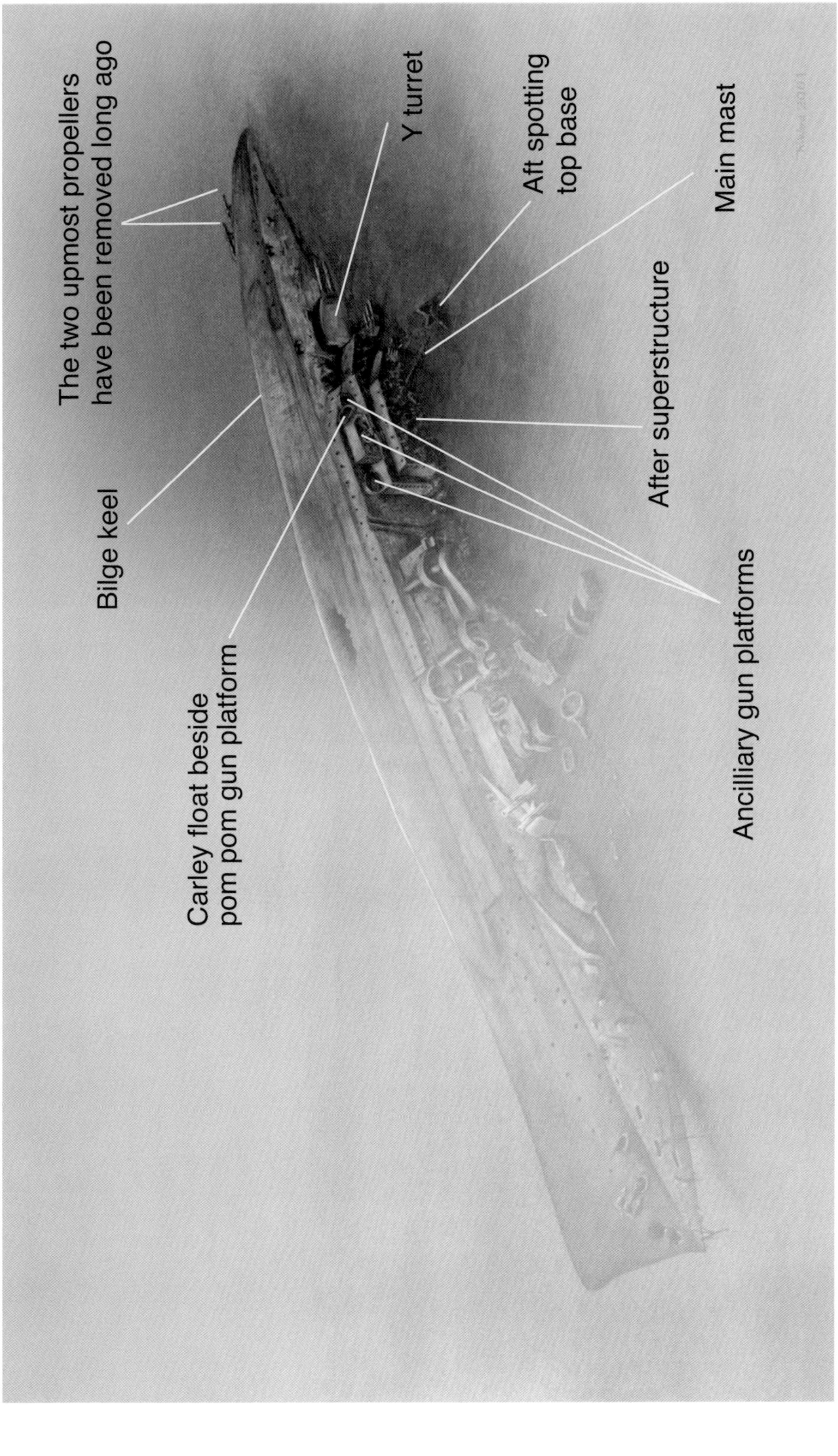

The two upmost propellers
have been removed long ago

Y turret

Aft spotting
top base

Main mast

Bilge keel

After superstructure

Carley float beside
pom pom gun platform

Ancilliary gun platforms

Stern section detail of HMS Repulse

Above: The rigging spreader and base for the main mast crow's nest lies on the seabed – its rigging tangled up and covered in sea life. © Author's collection

Below: Uppermost starboard-side prop shaft and strut.
© Guy Wallis

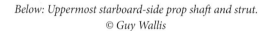

At the aft end of the bridge superstructure a Carley float is trapped beside an anti-aircraft machine gun platform. © Guy Wallis

The Royal Navy Ensign flown by the Tri-Services expedition flutters in the underwater breeze on HMS Repulse. © Guy Wallis

Bibliography

The Admiralty, Gunnery Branch. *The Gunnery Pocket Book*. B. R. 224/45. 1945.

Ash, Bernard. *Someone Had Blundered*. Doubleday & Co, 1961.

Attiwill, K. *Fortress: The Story of the Siege and Fall of Singapore*. Doubleday & Co, 1960.

Battleships of WWII. An International Encyclopedia. Arms & Armour Press, 1998.

Bennet, H. G. *Why Singapore Fell*. Angus & Robertson, 1944.

Bowden, Tim. *Changi Photographer – George Aspinall's Record of Captivity*. Times Editions, 1984.

Brooke, G. *Singapore's Dunkirk*. Pen & Sword Books Ltd, 1989.

Callahan, R. *The Worst Disaster: The Fall of Singapore*. The University of Delaware Press, 1977.

Chaphekar, S. G. *A Brief Study of the Malayan Campaign, 1941–42*. Bailey & Swinfern, 1960.

Chippington, G. *Singapore: The Inexcusable Betrayal*. The Self Publishing Association, 1992.

Churchill, W. S. *The Second World War*. Pimlico, 1948–54. New edition 2002.

Day, David. *The Great Betrayal: Britain, Australia and the Onset of the Pacific War, 1939–42*. OUP, 1988.

Elphick, P. *Singapore: The Pregnable Fortress*. Hodder & Stoughton, 1995.

Garzke, William H., Jr., Dulin, Robert O. Jr. & Denlay, Kevin V. *Death of a Battleship: The Loss of HMS* Prince of Wales. *A Marine Forensics Analysis of the Sinking*. Royal Institute of Naval Architects analysis, 2009 (available online at www.rina.org.uk).

Garzke, William H., Jr., Denlay, Kevin V. & Dulin, Robert O. Jr. *Death of a Battleship: a Re-analysis of the Tragic Loss of HMS* Prince of Wales. (members of the SNAME Marine Forensics Committee), 2012 (available online at www.explorers.org).

Gilchrist, A. *Malaya 1941: The Fall of a Fighting Empire*. Robert Hale Ltd, 1992.

Grenfell, Russell. *Main Fleet to Singapore*. Faber & Faber, 1951.

Hall, E. R. *Glory in Chaos: The RAAF in the Far East, 1940–42*. Sembawang Association, 1989.

Hase, G. von. *Kiel and Jutland*. Leonaur Ltd., 2011. First published 1923.

Heriot, Guy. *Changi Interlude. Leaves from the Diary of a Third Class Internee*. W. E. Baxter Ltd, 1946.

Hough, Richard. *The Hunting of Force Z: Britain's Greatest Modern Naval Disaster*. Collins, 1963.

Kinvig, C. *Scapegoat: General Percival of Singapore*. Brassey's (UK) Ltd, 1996.

Kirby, S. *Singapore: The Chain of Disaster*. Littlehampton Book Services, 1971.

Konstam, A. *British Battleships 1939–45* (2). Osprey Publishing, 2009.

Kratoska, P. *Singapore: The Battle that Changed the World*. James Leasor Ltd, 1998.

McCormack, Charles DCM. *You'll Die in Singapore,* Pan Books, 1954.

Middlebrook, M. & Mahoney, P. *Battleship. The Loss of the* Prince of Wales *and the* Repulse. Penguin Books, 1977.

Ministry of Defence. *The Loss of HMS* Prince of Wales *and* Repulse, *10 December 1941, Battle Summary No 14*.BR 1736(8)/1955, ADM 234/330. National Archives, Kew.

Nicholson, Arthur. *Hostages to Fortune: Winston Churchill and the Loss of the* Prince of Wales *and* Repulse. Phoenix Hill, 2005.

Percival, A. E. *The War in Malaya*. Eyre & Spottiswoode, 1949.

Prince of Wales. General Arrangement Plans No AF3 11.

Roberts, John & Raven, Alan. *British Battleships of WWII*. Arms & Armour Press, 1976.

Tarrant, V. *King George V Battleships*. Arms & Armour Press, 1991.

Tsuji, M. *Singapore: The Japanese Version*. Mayflower, 1960.

Warren, Alan. *Singapore 1942*, Talisman Publishing, 2002.